How United Methodists Study Scripture

How
$\mathcal{M}$ UNITED
ETHODISTS
Study
Scripture

Editor:
Gayle C. FELTON

Writers:
Catherine G. **GONZÁLEZ**
Ben **WITHERINGTON III**
C. Everett **TILSON**

ABINGDON PRESS/Nashville

HOW UNITED METHODISTS STUDY SCRIPTURE

Copyright © 1999 by Abingdon Press.

This book is printed on acid-free paper.

Unless otherwise noted, all of the Scripture quotations are from the New Revised Standard Version of the Bible, copyright © 1989 by the Division of Christian Education of the National Council of Churches of Christ in the USA. Used by permission.

Library of Congress Cataloging-in-Publication Data

González, Catherine Gunsalus.
    How United Methodists study scripture / writers, Catherine G. González, Ben Witherington, C. Everett Tilson : editor, Gayle C. Felton.
        p. cm.
    Includes bibliographical references.
    ISBN 0-687-08422-9 (pbk. : alk. paper)
        1. Bible—Study and teaching—United Methodist Church (U.S.)—History. 2. Bible—Study and teaching—United Methodist Church—History. I. Witherington, Ben, 1951- . II. Tilson, Everett. III. Felton, Gayle Carlton, 1942- . IV. Title.
BS588.U54G66 1999
220 ' .088 ' 27—dc21   98-50311
                                                                CIP

99 00 01 02 03 04 05 06 07 08—10 9 8 7 6 5 4 3 2

MANUFACTURED IN THE UNITED STATES OF AMERICA

To John Alan,
my grandson

Contents

Introduction

UNITED METHODISTS understand ourselves as a Bible-valuing people. Perhaps no qualification for a potential pastor is so widely expressed by laity as that he or she "preach the Bible." Theological school leaders attest that the admonition they hear most frequently is to "teach those students the Bible." The sharpest criticism made of our denomination's curriculum materials in the past was that they were "not biblical." Questions about matters of belief and practice eventually boil down to the question "what does the Bible say about it?"

The phenomenal popularity of the DISCIPLE Bible study program since 1986 is concrete evidence of the eagerness of our people to participate in scriptural study and reflection. In a recent study of six mainline Protestant denominations, United Methodist adults expressed at least slightly more interest in Bible study than did their counterparts in other denominations, with the sole exception of the Southern Baptist Convention. Indeed, 78 percent of the United Methodist adults surveyed ranked learning about the Bible as the subject in which they had the greatest interest.[1] Some indication of how United Methodists view the Bible may also be found in this study. Fifty-four percent of those questioned in the eighty-seven participating United Methodist congregations agreed with the statement that the Bible was "inspired by God and recorded by writers who interpreted God's message in the context of their times." Only 7 percent said that it was "dictated by God word for word and recorded by writers not influenced by their times."[2]

The issue of how United Methodists study and interpret the Bible is at the crux of many of the major points of discussion in the denomination today. In our disputes and controversies, all of us attempt to wrap our views securely in the mantle of carefully selected biblical texts that appear to justify our positions. The truth is that we all recognize "a canon within the canon." We differ largely in what we select as our own version of canon and in our willingness to acknowledge its existence. Our inclination to exploit Scripture by using it as a weapon against those with whom we disagree threatens to dishonor biblical truth. Our desire to learn and be guided by God's Word is requisite to faithfulness as individuals and as a community of God's people.

Since the formation of The United Methodist Church in 1968, the issue of biblical authority has been discussed. In 1972, a section entitled "Our Theological Task" was added to the *Discipline* to address the question of how United Methodists are to think and decide theologically. In this statement, the sources and criteria of Scripture, tradition, experience, and reason were said to constitute a "Wesleyan quadrilateral" of theological authority. Many in the church felt that this statement failed to make clear that Scripture was to be valued above the other points of the quadrilateral. Consequently the theological statement adopted in 1988[3] and appearing in the *Disciplines* since then, clarified that "Scripture, as the constitutive witness to the wellsprings of our faith, occupies a place of primary authority among these theological sources." The other three points of the quadrilateral are not discarded: "Wesley believed that the living core of the Christian faith was revealed in Scripture, illumined by tradition, vivified in personal experience, and confirmed by reason." But, the preeminent role of the Bible is plainly affirmed: "Scripture is primary, revealing the Word of

God 'so far as it is necessary for our salvation.' Therefore, our theological task, in both its critical and constructive aspects, focuses on disciplined study of the Bible."[4]

In the chapters that constitute this book, four authors with different emphases contribute to this process of "disciplined study of the Bible."

Catherine Gunsalus González summarizes the roles of the Bible in the periods of the early church, the early and later Middle Ages, and the Protestant Reformation. She deals cogently with matters of scriptural authority and interpretation during the first sixteen centuries of the Christian church.

Ben Witherington III concentrates on the study and interpretation of the Bible in early Methodism in both England and America. Through analysis of the work of John Wesley, Francis Asbury, and Richard Watson, he identifies some aspects that were characteristic of our tradition in the eighteenth and nineteenth centuries.

Issues of contemporary scriptural study and interpretation are addressed by Everett Tilson. He underlines the significance of the historical context in all approaches to understanding revelation, canonization, and interpretation.

My concluding chapter attempts to investigate what are and/or should be some distinctively United Methodist features of biblical study and interpretation.

As you read this book, and as we all continue our reading and study of God's Word, may we be guided by Charles Wesley's poem based on 2 Corinthians 3:5-6:

> Whether the Word be preached or read,
> no saving benefit I gain
> from empty sounds or letters dead;
> unprofitable all and vain,
> unless by faith thy word I hear
> and see its heavenly character.

Unmixed with faith, the Scripture gives
no comfort, life, or light to see
but me in darker darkness leaves,
implunged in deeper misery,
overwhelmed with nature's sorest ills.
The Spirit saves, the letter kills.

If God enlighten through his Word,
I shall my kind Enlightener bless;
but void and naked of my Lord,
what are all the verbal promises?
Nothing to me, till faith divine
inspire, inspeak, and make them mine.

Jesus, the appropriating grace
'tis thine on sinners to bestow.
Open mine eyes to see thy face,
open my heart thyself to know.
And then I through thy Word obtain
sure present, and eternal gain.[5]

—Gayle Carlton Felton

Chapter 1

Reading the Bible in the First Sixteen Centuries

Catherine Gunsalus GONZÁLEZ

For THE FIRST fifteen centuries of the church's life, most Christians would have been puzzled if asked how they read the Bible. Most did not read it. Yet during much of this time, especially in the first five centuries, the average church member's knowledge of the Scriptures was probably far higher than it is today. We must therefore ask two questions. First, why did they not read the Bible? Second, how did they come to learn what the Bible said?

The Early Church

We take for granted two things the ancient world could not assume: a high rate of literacy and cheap books. Estimates of the literacy rate for the Roman Empire at the time of the Christian church's beginning vary from 5 to 15 percent, dependent almost entirely on social status and occupation.[1] Since the church was composed of far more persons from the lower echelons of society, one can assume that the literacy rate within the church was not more than this. In addition to the lack of literacy among those whose language was one of the ancient languages within the Empire—Greek, Latin, Aramaic, Coptic—here were also groups within the Empire and on its borders whose language did not exist in written form. Theirs were oral cultures. In many of these cases, it was the missionaries of the church who developed a written language for the people so that Scripture and worship materials could be translated. Under these circumstances, literacy was very limited among the common people.

Another factor was the cost of writing materials. Paper was made out of papyrus and, later, parchments. Both were expensive. A single sheet would cost the equivalent of about thirty dollars today.[2] Obviously, such expensive materials were out of the reach of the vast majority. The cost of paper and the lack of literacy are related. Imagine how much a book would cost if it had to be handwritten and basic materials were so expensive. If books cannot be obtained, what is the purpose of learning to read? Less expensive writing materials were available—pottery shards, clay tablets—that might be used for household or minor commercial purposes, but if lower social classes needed such records, they probably used the services of a public scribe. They themselves did not have to be literate. Wax tablets were used for temporary notes, even for the wealthy.

The expense of books also limited access to the Bible for congregations. Books were very precious items; a copy of Scripture was a treasure for a congregation. Furthermore, such parchment manuscripts would be in several volumes, not the simple book we have today. A congregation might have some of their own members go to a neighboring church to copy a portion of the Scripture they did not already possess. Since in the first few centuries the church generally met in houses, there might be several house churches in one city, but only the central congregation, where all house churches met on Sunday, probably possessed the treasured copy of Scripture.

The written word was extremely important for the

church. The Scripture, letters from one church to another dealing with common issues that needed to be worked out together and essays written to refute heresies and clarify what the church taught, all were absolutely essential for the life of the church. All had to be meticulously copied in order to be preserved. The leadership of the church had to be literate. In fact, for many, the preparation for ordained ministry in the church began with the office of "lector" or "reader." Before the congregation's worship began, the lector read portions of Scripture for an hour or more as people gathered. Until the end of the second century, "Scripture" meant the Old Testament, but the lector also read from letters and "the memoirs of the apostles," which we assume means the Gospels. Justin Martyr wrote: "And on the day that is called Sunday, all who live in cities or in the country gather together in one place, and the memoirs of the apostles or the writings of the prophets are read, as long as time permits."[3] In this predominantly oral culture, there was an emphasis on memorizing biblical texts, even among those who could read.

Within the worship service, Scripture played a major part. Not only were portions read as the basis for the sermon, Psalms were also sung by the congregation, and therefore readily memorized. Beyond this, the life of the church was woven into particular texts. Easter was associated with the story of the Exodus and the crossing of the Jordan into the Promised Land. Baptisms rehearsed Noah and the ark and Jonah's return to faithfulness after his time in the water. The church year developed partly as a means to have the congregation live through the major events of the Gospel narrative, from the expectation of the Messiah, his birth, baptism, ministry, betrayal, death, resurrection, and ascension, to the sending of the Holy Spirit. Every year the church was reminded of these events in its worship. The lessons for these seasons became familiar and therefore memorized. There is an account in a letter of Saint Augustine in the early fifth century about a bishop in North Africa who read a new translation of the text of Jonah in the worship service. The congregation shouted out the version they were used to and refused to let the bishop continue until the familiar version was used.

In addition to liturgy as a means of learning the content of Scripture, there was the role of the "the rule of faith." The rule of faith was the brief statement of the gospel message that was similar in every church, though not identical. What we know as "The Apostles' Creed" is a form of the rule of faith used in Rome and in most of the Western part of the church. Its major use was as a baptismal confession. Every member knew the rule of faith and was taught the meaning of it. A bishop in Gaul in the late second century wrote that even Christians whose native language was not a written one knew the basic content of Scripture because they knew the rule of faith. The bishop also said that these groups could readily spot heretical teaching because they knew the rule. Bishop Irenaeus wrote:[4]

> [M]any nations of those barbarians who believe in Christ do assent, having salvation written in their hearts by the Spirit, without paper or ink, and carefully preserving the ancient tradition, believing in one God, the Creator of heaven and earth. . . . Those who, in absence of written documents, have believed this faith, are barbarians, so far as regards our language; but as regards doctrine, manner, and tenor of life, they are, because of faith, very wise indeed. . . . If any one were to preach to these men the inventions of the heretics, speaking to them in their own language, they would at once stop their ears, and flee as far off as possible.

Heresies were rampant in the second, third, and fourth centuries. Among the major issues were: Whether the God of Israel was the God of Jesus, or an inferior one? Could a good God create material reality, or only spiritual reality? Was Jesus really human? Was he born? Did he really die? Was Jesus

16

God, or a human adopted by God? Was Jesus a second God? Are Christians monotheistic or do they worship two Gods? All of these questions were addressed by the rule of faith.

As this list of heresies makes clear, a major issue for early Christians was the relationship between the God of Israel and Jesus. This meant also the relation of the Old Testament and the New. Some of the heresies simply said Christians should not use the Old Testament. In addition, some created their own gospels that denied Jesus was truly human. Others used some parts of the New Testament but eliminated all references to the Old Testament. In response to such views, the church formed its own canon—the list of books that should be accepted as Scripture. They included the Old Testament, the four Gospels, the letters of Paul, and the other books that we know as the New Testament. They excluded the later gospels that denied the real humanity of Jesus, especially his birth and his death. This process was generally complete by the end of the second century.

Against heretical views, the church constantly insisted upon the relationship of the two testaments. They did this in two major ways. First, ancient writers frequently included lists of prophecies in the Old Testament that were fulfilled by Jesus. Some passages on these lists of prophecies may seem very far-fetched to us, but this itself is evidence of the strongly felt need to make such a connection. Other passages are insightful and familiar to us. God promised to be faithful, and in Christ this promise is fulfilled. God promised to come among the people as their savior and shepherd. Jesus was, and is, this savior and shepherd. God promised to send a messiah at the end of the age. In Jesus, this happened.

A second way of linking the Old and New Testaments was by means of what is called *typology*. This method found patterns in the way God related to humanity in general and the people of God in particular, showing the consistency of God in the Old and New Testaments. Some of these "types" also would be strange to us, but others are very instructive. For instance, God fed the people when they were in the wilderness with bread from heaven. In the Gospel of John (6:30-38), Jesus refers to himself as the bread of heaven. Holy Communion is also the bread of heaven, given to God's people as strength for their journey. In the Exodus from Egypt, God freed the Hebrews from slavery. In the cross and the Resurrection of Jesus, God freed all people from bondage to sin, death, and the power of evil. In the Flood, God exercised judgment on the world, saving the few righteous in the ark so that they were not killed by the water. In baptism (1 Peter 3:18-21), God frees from judgment those who enter the ark of the church, bringing them safely through the waters of baptism. It is no accident that many of these typologies are connected with the liturgical life of the church, since the assumption is that the pattern of divine acts is being celebrated in the present service of worship. The congregation found itself living the meaning of Scripture, thereby reinforcing its understanding of the biblical passage. Ancient Christian art that has been preserved shows this typological use of Scripture. For instance, images of the ark and of Jonah appear on early baptisteries.

A third method, called *allegory,* was popular in areas of the church strongly influenced by Greek philosophy. This method often found secret meanings, almost a code, in particular words of Scripture. It also found spiritual meanings in historical passages that were otherwise difficult to interpret. For instance, God's command to destroy towns in Canaan during the conquest was understood as not really an order to destroy actual people, but rather a command that we should put to death in ourselves all evil desires.

In the late fourth and early fifth centuries, Saint Jerome translated the Bible from its original languages into Latin. Later called the Vulgate, this version was widely used in the Western church. There had been earlier Latin versions, but the Vulgate was based on the Hebrew text of the Old Testament, rather than the Greek translations usually used.

Jerome also wrote a number of biblical commentaries. In them he shows another method of interpretation. He stressed the historical context and meaning of various passages and avoided the extremes of the allegorical method. Though this would not have great effect in the Middle Ages, it would be a very important tradition in the West later, particularly at the time of the Reformation.

The Early Medieval Church

After the fourth century, life changed drastically for the church, particularly in the West. Two major factors were responsible. First, in the early fourth century, the Emperor Constantine stopped the persecution and began, instead, to support the church. By the end of the fourth century, Christianity was the dominant religion of the Empire, and all other public worship was prohibited, except for Judaism, which was tolerated but not supported.

Once almost everyone was a Christian and the church was closely allied with the structures and power of the state, worship became much more a production by the clergy than an involvement of the whole people. Baptism was more an expected rite of passage for newborns, rather than the dramatic addition of converts who joined the church in spite of the possibility of persecution. Until this time, preparation for membership in the church was accomplished through the *catechumenate*—a two-to-three-year period of spiritual, ethical, and intellectual formation. Teachers were in charge of these groups, and the process was fairly rigorous. Catechumens attended the worship services of the church, at least for the reading of Scripture and the sermon. They were dismissed before the Lord's Supper. Much of the time in the catechumenate was spent on ethical and moral issues, showing the difference between the demands of the Christian life and the usual life in the Roman Empire. Only after it was judged that candidates were ready to lead this new life were they baptized. Once Constantine had shown great favor to the church, there was no more fear of persecution. Many people sought to join the Christian community, more because it was supported by the emperor than from clear conviction. There were so many who sought to enter that there were not enough teachers for them. Fairly quickly, the time of preparation shrank and eventually most people were born into the Christian community. Unfortunately though, many had little real understanding of any difference between the church and the world, or the Christian life and any other life, except for certain ceremonies peculiar to the church. Christian education and formation of the congregation lost ground enormously at this time. In fact, it would be true to say that the church in the West has not adequately done its own education since the fourth century. It has depended upon the wider culture, since it was considered to be a Christian culture, to do the vast majority of the education. The amount of time spent with the worshiping congregation or with the teachers in preparation for baptism decreased greatly. Daily worship and teaching, with some meals together, gave way to a few hours a week on Sunday. The church had less and less opportunity to shape the lives and form the characters of its members, even though its numbers had increased enormously.

The connection between patterns in Scripture and the church's worship—typology—was generally lost. Still, the rule of faith and the observance of important times in the church year continued to be major devices for teaching the basic outline of the gospel story.

A second factor was the invasion and destruction of the western, or Latin, part of the Roman Empire by the Germanic tribes. The first sack of Rome was in 410. Thereafter, wave after wave of invasions swept through. Huns, Goths, Vandals, Franks, and Lombards surged across Europe during the fifth and sixth centuries. Later centuries would bring Angles, Saxons, Normans, and Slavs who would add to the population. One effect of these invasions was the destruction of the stable society that had existed with governmental and educational structures. The city of Rome had a population of about a million at its height at the beginning of the second century. By the end of the seventh century, the population was down to about thirty thousand.[5]

The church was the major institution able to provide some very basic services. Missionaries translated the Scripture into the languages of these new groups of people in Europe. Often it was necessary to create a written form of a language in order to do so and then train indigenous church leadership to be literate in it. Increasingly, art forms in the churches portrayed significant passages from the Bible, and pageants tied to the celebrations of the church year conveyed the major narrative, especially of the life of Jesus. Plays based on other biblical stories were also popular.

The language of the Roman Catholic Church was Latin. In the southern part of Europe where the old Empire had existed, Latin was generally understood by those whose language was gradually shifting to what we know as Romance languages today. However, in the northern areas, the Germanic languages were so different from Latin, that for many people the language of the church and their own mother tongue bore little resemblance to each other. We cannot fault the church completely for this situation. The Germanic languages were not unified, which meant that one could travel a relatively short distance and have difficulty being understood. Latin provided a unity throughout the church that made education possible across a wide geographical area, as well as manuscripts that could be read all over the emerging European culture. Education implied knowing Latin.

The Scripture and liturgies used were in Latin. No longer did Christians gather long before the service to hear the Scripture read. They probably would not have understood what they heard anyway. People came for the ceremonies. For most of the period from the seventh to the twelfth century, many Christians would have to rely on the creed, the celebrations of the church year, plays, and church art to convey the biblical message in ways that they could grasp.

Preaching was not common in many areas, and often the parish priests were not educated. There were attempts to remedy this situation by the creation of schools for clergy, but further invasions ended such projects. There is no reason to believe that literacy had increased among lay people generally from the earlier period, nor that the price of writing materials and books had decreased. For those who were literate in their native language and who could afford such purchases, there were some religious books in the Germanic languages, but few could use them.

All was not bleak in the early medieval period, however. Often it has been referred to as "the Dark Ages" because of the invasions and consequent social chaos. But at the same time, there were many hidden developments that were the basis for later significant progress. Though lay people, and even priests in many parishes, might be losing the knowledge of Scripture that those of earlier periods managed to have, the monastic movement in the West developed rapidly after the work of Saint Benedict in the fifth century. Benedictine monasticism was flourishing and was the real center of what learning was available. Monastics learned to read Latin sufficiently to carry out their tasks of singing the Psalms, which were sung through every two weeks or so. Eight times a day they gathered for worship. During the course of the year they memorized many passages of Scripture. Many monastics copied manuscripts—work that also demanded a knowledge of Latin. The Bible was the chief, though not the only, manuscript they copied. Monastics—both men and women— read and knew Scripture. So within the early medieval period there were really two levels of the reading and the knowledge of Scripture: poor among the vast majority of people in local churches including many priests, increasingly good among monastics.

Irish monasticism was a separate and significant movement. It developed independent of Benedictine forms and in isolation from the rest of Europe. Ireland was not invaded until the tenth century, so there was a long period of relative peace and security. Through the introduction of Christianity, the Irish language developed a written form. Monasteries became centers of learning even more than on the Continent. Greek was studied in Irish monasteries while the knowledge of Greek was lost in Western Europe. The ancient tradition of storytelling bards was combined with monasticism to make the keepers of the people's tradition honored persons in the wider community. Furthermore, monasteries were the centers of towns and villages rather than being isolated. Irish monasticism also maintained a practice of missions, sending monks to Scotland, England, and the Continent to found monasteries that maintained this tradition of learning. When the invasions were finally over, it was to these monasteries that Europe would turn to reintroduce a significant knowledge of the church's own past, including a knowledge of the Scripture.

The Later Middle Ages

By the end of the eleventh century, the invasions were over. Western Europe was becoming a stable, increasingly unified society. In essence, Europe was beginning and the church was a major factor in this development. Partly as a result of the crusades that began at the end of the eleventh century, commerce and trade increased; cities were founded or reestablished; and there was trade with the Middle East, including products from the Far East. As commercial classes grew, so did literacy and wealth among those who were neither scholars nor nobles. But these people often did not read Latin. By the fourteenth and fifteenth centuries, there would be an increasing demand for books in the vernacular, or common, languages. There would also be pressure for translations of the Bible into popular languages. In England, Wycliffe and Tyndale are the names associated with this effort. John Wycliffe was a fourteenth-century scholar who believed that much of the church's traditional practice and theology contradicted Scripture. He therefore believed that Scripture ought to be in the language of the people so that they could know the truth. He sent out preachers to proclaim what Scripture taught, preaching in the vernacular. Wycliffe's followers became known as the Lollards, who were considered heretical by the Roman Catholic Church because some of the doctrines they proclaimed were radically distinct from Catholic teaching. In the sixteenth century, shortly after Luther published his German translation, William Tyndale translated the first printed Bible in English, beginning with the New Testament in 1526.

Schools developed in the growing cities, taking away from the monasteries the leadership in learning. In the twelfth century these schools coalesced into universities. These were very large institutions, with growing numbers of students in each. Major ones were in Paris, Oxford, and Bologna. Educational opportunities greatly expanded, at least for those who knew Latin. Latin was the language of the university. It was the unifying factor for students from all over Europe whose native tongues were the vernacular languages. Lectures, examinations, discussions, and books were in Latin. There continued to be a gap between the ability to read and understand Scripture among university-educated priests and those who served the laity in parishes, especially in rural areas. Universities were under the rule of the church, so only clergy attended. But those priests who served in small churches had no such educational advantages. Poorly educated clergy, unable to read Scripture, meant poorly educated laity.

Within the universities there was indeed a study of Scripture. In the works of the greatest theologian of the thirteenth century, Thomas Aquinas, it is clear that he is well acquainted with the Bible. In addition to his studies, he was a Dominican monk. But, it is also clear that the Bible is one part of Christian tradition and does not have authority over all other traditions passed down through the church.

In the late fourteenth and fifteenth centuries, there were rapid developments in technology that led to increases in literacy. From Chinese influence two inventions found their way into European use. The first was paper made from rags. It was far cheaper than any writing material previously available. Since it was so much thinner, it also made books smaller. The second was the movable type printing press. The combination meant that books now could be created far more cheaply than before. In addition, a new monastic group, the Brethren of the Common Life, began basic education for the children of the rising commercial classes. These schools were conducted in the vernacular, not in Latin. These were day schools for boys and for girls. This education was necessary for commercial classes, giving them the ability to keep records and accounts. Since these were usually family businesses, wives and husbands were involved and needed such education. The Brethren of the Common Life were also concerned to teach piety, and with this education they communicated a basic knowledge of Scripture. At many points they opposed the corruption of the church of their day on the basis of the gospel. They influenced many of the reformers of the sixteenth century, on both the Protestant and the Catholic sides.

The Reformation Period

It is difficult to imagine the Protestant Reformation occurring without the ready availability of printing, relatively inexpensive paper, significant rates of literacy, and books in the languages of the common people. In addition, there were increasing numbers of people who could afford books. These are developments, which although secular in themselves, significantly affected the reading of Scripture. Such factors would not necessarily have increased the reading of the Bible had they not been combined with the issues of the Reformation itself.

What were these issues? Protestants objected to traditions that had become central to medieval Roman Catholic life, but had little or no foundation in Scripture nor in the early life of the church. Had the leadership of the church not been corrupt, the situation might have been resolved differently. However, in the fifteenth and sixteenth centuries, in the cultural ethos of the Renaissance, many in the church's leadership in Rome were concerned with supporting the artistic endeavors of that movement. These endeavors were financed by monies raised through highly suspect means. For instance, church offices such as a bishop and an archbishop were often given to those who agreed to pay for them, even though the person was totally unqualified for the office, and in fact might even be a child. "Indulgences" could be purchased that drew on the excess good deeds of the saints—that is deeds done beyond what was deemed necessary for their own salvation. This "treasury of merit" would then count for someone else, either living or dead, for whom the indulgence was purchased. This practice was based on the idea that we must earn our salvation, though the church, established by Christ, provided the means for grace that supplemented what we were able to do. This grace was received primarily through the sacraments, but indulgences added to it. Money raising was involved in many actions of the church, even some of the sacraments. All of this was justified by the undisputed authority of the church to decide what was required for salvation.

Against this view, Protestants asserted that only Scripture could define what was needed for salvation. The tradition of the church and the hierarchy of the church did not have this authority. Though for Martin Luther the starting point was the issue of indulgences, the implications were much more far-reaching. Issues such as the Lenten fast, meatless Fridays, celibate clergy, even monastic life itself, were traditions that, judged by Scripture, were found to be unsupported. The phrase that became the watchword of Protestants—*sola scriptura*: Scripture alone—meant that the ultimate authority for the church is Scripture. Church tradition is not such an authority, nor is the leadership of the church.

The Bible in Protestantism

If the Bible is the primary and final authority, then obviously Protestants were going to stress a knowledge of Scripture as absolutely essential in the life of the church. Furthermore, Protestants emphasized that not only should the leadership of the church know Scripture well, but also all members should study the Bible. This was not only for the sake of their own religious life, though that was very important. It was also so that they could be vigilant lest the church again substitute human ideas for the Word of God. This meant that translations into vernacular languages should be advocated, as well as cheaply printed Bibles, so that every family could have a copy. Obviously, this also promoted literacy among Protestants. Partly as a result of the Renaissance, Protestants also demanded translations from the original languages—Hebrew and Greek—rather than from the Latin Vulgate of Jerome. The Roman Catholic Church did not encourage translations, but did permit them, as long as they were from the Vulgate and had footnotes that explained any passages that might easily be misinterpreted by the laity. The laity were not encouraged to read the Bible. In Protestant areas, translations into vernacular languages abounded, beginning with Luther's translation into German.

Protestant churches insisted on preaching on a portion of the Bible that was read aloud. In many Protestant churches, the sermon became the central focus of the service, and the sacraments took a clearly secondary place. Preaching required the study of a biblical text and the expounding of it so that it became a living word in the lives of the hearers. It was not simply the communication of past events, but the Word of God for the present moment. This was the chief task of pastors. Calvin wrote:

> This is the extent of the power with which the pastors of the Church, by whatever name they may be distinguished, ought to be invested;—that by the word of God they may venture to do all things with confidence; may constrain all the strength, glory, wisdom and pride of the world to obey and submit to his majesty; supported by his power, may govern all mankind, from the highest to the lowest; may build up the house of Christ, and subvert the house of Satan; may feed the sheep, and drive away the wolves; may instruct and exhort the docile; may reprove, rebuke, and restrain the rebellious and obstinate; may bind and loose; may discharge their lightnings and thunders, if necessary; but all in the word of God.[6]

The Interpretation of Scripture

It sounds quite simple: Scripture, not tradition, is the final authority for the church. That is a basic Protestant principle. However, it is neither as clear nor as simple as it sounds. There are two particular problems that rapidly appeared within Protestant circles. First, on what issues is Scripture the final authority? For the sixteenth century, the particular concern was worship. Should the worship of the church conform to New Testament worship? Should organs be used, for instance, though they were not used in the New

28

Testament? Should there be hymns whose words are not from the Bible? How ought baptisms to be done? How much water? At what age? How are we to understand the presence of Christ in the Lord's Supper? How often should it be served? The problem was that the New Testament was not written as a manual for worship, so the answers to such basic questions were not spelled out clearly. Later the question would arise as to whether Scripture was to be the final authority on history and science, and this would create serious debates among Protestants. Scripture might be claimed as the ultimate standard, but there was much debate as to what issues were subject to biblical authority. For most Protestants, it was clear that Scripture was the ultimate authority at least on matters of faith: what Christians were to believe, and morals: what Christians were to do.

The second major problem was who had the authority to decide what it was that Scripture taught? For instance, did *sola scriptura* mean that individual Christians were to interpret Scripture for themselves, without regard for the rest of the church's interpretation? For both Martin Luther and John Calvin the answer to this question was clearly "no." The Lutheran and the Reformed churches (the Reformed churches are those stemming from the Swiss Reformation, whose major leaders were Ulrich Zwingli and John Calvin) both quickly became *confessional churches.* This means that as a whole church they worked out fairly lengthy documents that gave a systematic statement of what they understood Scripture to say about the meaning of the Christian faith. For Lutherans, the one confession is the Augsburg Confession. For the Reformed churches, there are several, generally created by national churches, in Scotland, Switzerland, Holland, England, and others. The most famous in English-speaking churches is the Westminster Confession. The Reformed churches have amended and added confessions throughout the years. In confessional churches, those who are ordained are usually required to affirm their agreement with the confessional standards of the church. This means that though Scripture is the ultimate authority in the church, there is an agreed-upon interpretation of Scripture. It is possible within Reformed churches to alter these confessional statements if it is decided they are counter to the Bible on some issue, but this is usually a difficult process. Within the Lutheran churches it has been almost impossible to alter the Augsburg Confession. How then are we to say that tradition has no role to play as an authority in Protestant churches?

Beginning with Martin Luther, a new form of printed resource also provided a major method of Christian education. This was the *catechism*. Catechisms are fairly brief summaries of the faith done in simple language, in question and answer form. They reflect the theological stance of the church producing them. Originally intended for children, they were the foundation for communicating the faith to the whole congregation. These catechisms could be printed very cheaply so that every family could have a copy. In Geneva, parents were expected to attend a Sunday afternoon service with their children when specific questions of the catechism were explained. Then, during the week, the parents could help their children study and perhaps memorize the answers to the questions for that week. This provided education for the parents as well as for the children. This knowledge then created the context within which the family read the Scripture at home. The catechisms often contained interpretations of the Apostles' Creed, the Lord's Prayer, and the Ten Commandments and more general information such as the role of Scripture, the nature of faith, the sacraments, the church, and salvation. Catechisms were such a valuable resource that the Roman Catholic Church began issuing its own form, since basic Christian education was a need there as well.

We have mentioned the two confessional church traditions: the Lutheran and the Reformed. There were two other families of churches that emerged in the Reformation period. These were the Anglican (or Episcopal) and the Anabaptist. The Anglican Church retained a stress on the authority of tradition, but generally limited it to the tradition of the early church, eliminating the issues created by the medieval tradition. The Anabaptists represent what is often called the radical wing of the Reformation. The major groups were German-speaking ones that held to believer's baptism only, rejected involvement with the state, were pacifists, and assumed that any true church would be persecuted. Their descendants in our own day are the Mennonites, Amish, and Brethren churches. They held that church practices should duplicate what is found in the New Testament. Children who grew up in any one of these four church families generally continued in that church, reading the Bible through the lens of that church. It is therefore difficult to separate the power of tradition in Protestant reading of Scripture, though every church agreed that new understandings based on the Bible took precedence over tradition.

Protestants generally rejected allegorical methods of biblical interpretation because they allowed interpreters free rein to read into the text what they wished to find there. The historical method was the dominant form. In fact, it is particularly clear in the commentaries of John Calvin that the new university study of law greatly influenced the Protestant approach to biblical interpretation. Law was one of the major areas of study in the universities, and Calvin had studied law and theology. The study of law included tracing it back to its roots in ancient Roman law. It studied the language of the original law, showing the particular meaning of words in their ancient context. This was followed by a history of how the law had been interpreted in various later contexts. Then a summary of the meaning of the law was given, followed by a discussion of its present significance. Calvin followed this method in his biblical commentaries. He translated the particular text from the original language, did a study of the significant words and their nuances in the original language, showed significant elements of the history of the interpretation of the text in the church as seen by earlier theologians, gave a summary of what he believed the passage meant in its own setting, and then showed how it applied to the life of the church in his own day. Calvin's commentaries provided a model for the Protestant sermon. Tradition had a role in his biblical interpretation, but it was not a controlling factor.

By the late sixteenth century, Protestants were beginning to deal with an issue that would continue to be a major debate in the next several centuries. In fact, it remains a point of discussion within churches and between denominations. Is Scripture readily understandable to anyone who reads it regardless of the state of their faith, or does it require the inner working of the Holy Spirit for someone to comprehend its meaning? What is the relationship of the printed text of the Bible and the work of the Holy Spirit? If there is great stress on Scripture, does it mean that the Holy Spirit is unnecessary? If there is great stress on the Holy Spirit, does it mean that the biblical text is not needed? The question only begins to arise in the immediate Reformation period. In fact, the same reformers can often be cited on both sides of what later will become a serious controversy. In the next two centuries, Protestant Orthodoxy—stressing Scripture—and Pietism—stressing the work of the Spirit—will show the different emphases. The seeds for this lie within the Reformation itself, though at the time, there was strong affirmation of the connection. Both the text and the Spirit are needed.

We can see that though Protestants held to Scripture alone as their authority, this did not solve all of the problems. How the various understandings worked out in practice is best seen through the example of a particular issue.

The Example of the Sacraments

Protestants who live centuries after the initial events that produced their churches often do not realize the enormous decisions that had to be made once the separation from the Roman Catholic Church occurred. The leaders looked to Scripture, but it was not always a simple task. Let us take one very clear example.

At the point of Luther's break with Rome in 1520, the Roman Catholic Church held that there were seven sacraments. This had been finally decided in the early thirteenth century after centuries of varying opinions on the subject. There had not been controversies, but rather there had been a lack of clarity as to what was a sacrament and therefore what should be counted. The seven sacraments of the Roman Catholic Church were (and still are): Baptism, Eucharist (the Lord's Supper), confirmation, penance and reconciliation, anointing of the sick, ordination, and marriage. There is no statement in the Bible that defines what a sacrament is or how many sacraments there are. Protestants agreed that Jesus instituted baptism and Eucharist, but there is no great agreement after that.

The Anabaptist groups rejected the term *sacrament* and instead used words like *ordinance*. Some also read in the Gospel of John (13:1-16) that Jesus instituted a third ordinance and commanded his followers to continue it. That was ceremonial foot washing. The Anabaptists therefore began that as a required practice in the church. They considered churches that did not perform foot washing as unbiblical in their practices. The rest of the Protestants rejected the necessity of foot washing. Their reasons were partly that there was no evidence, even in the New Testament and definitely not in the early church, that the church ever practiced it, though there is ample evidence that they baptized and celebrated the Lord's Supper. Were the

Anabaptists correct that the biblical text gives both warrant and command for foot washing in John 13? Were the other Protestants correct that the lived tradition of the church has substantial authority in the matter?

Luther considered *penance,* that is, sacramental confession of sins, to be of great comfort and importance. He had found it so when he was a troubled young monk. There was power in making confession in the presence of another human being, and there was reality in hearing the words of forgiveness spoken. He felt that Christians should confess their sins, not to a priest, but to other Christians and hear the gospel message of forgiveness from them. This is part of what he understood by "the priesthood of all believers." He could read in James 5:16: "Confess your sins to one another." But was this confession a sacrament? He debated the issue with himself and came to the conclusion that though it was a practice to be seriously encouraged, to make it a sacrament would take away from the meaning of baptism. Baptism is the seal of God's promise of forgiveness, renewed and activated by faith in God's promises to us. Penance would then be part of that renewal, but not a separate sacrament, as though God's promise at our baptism had been lost. On this basis, Luther decided there were only two sacraments.

John Calvin seriously considered ordination as a possible sacrament, since ordination signified the church's recognition that God continued to call people to proclaim God's Word. The ordained ministry was to him God's great gift to the church for the purpose of proclaiming the gospel in their midst. But Calvin decided that it should not be thought of as a sacrament, because a sacrament by definition should be something all Christians can receive, not something only a few obtain. Calvin believed that the New Testament did not give full directions for the church's life. He wrote:

> Because, in external discipline and ceremonies, he [the Lord] has not been pleased to give us minute directions what

we ought to do in every particular case, foreseeing that this would depend on different circumstances of different periods, and knowing that one form would not be adapted to all ages,—here we must have recourse to the general rules which he has given.[7]

At the same time, Calvin believed that only God could establish a sacrament, since it was a seal of God's promise to us. For those reasons, he agreed that there were only two sacraments.

In all of these debates, one can see that Scripture did not easily answer the questions being asked. Yet for all the churches, it was with Scripture that they had to struggle because it was their ultimate authority.

Conclusion

By the end of the Reformation, there were several issues upon which Protestants agreed and which distinguished them from Roman Catholics of the time. Scripture as the ultimate authority for church beliefs was central, although exactly how tradition was related to this was not clear. For none of the churches did *sola scriptura* mean individuals should interpret Scripture for themselves without regard for the wider church. In fact, the issue of tradition was for many Protestants the question of how wide was the community of faith which one should consider? Did it include those who had died centuries before? For some groups, confessions of faith were the distillation of the community's theological understanding of the teachings of Scripture, to which the leadership must adhere. The Reformation churches were not affected by the individualism that is typical of more modern congregations. At the same time, Scripture in the hands of the faithful, in their own language, was seen as a powerful defense against the danger of corrupt clergy who might lead the church astray.

Several new methods of Christian education were developed, thanks to the printing press. Catechisms were chief among these. The printing press also allowed biblical commentaries by great theologians to be in the hands of pastors, helping them in the task of preaching. Preaching was the dominant feature of Protestant worship. There were debates as to whether Scripture that was not to be preached on should even be read in the service. The sermon was a teaching device, but it was also in itself the Word of God at the moment. It was as though the word on the printed page of the Bible was the potential Word of God, but not fully that until it took form in the sermon for the life of the congregation that was gathered. The task of the preacher was a divine calling, and therefore pulpits were guarded against unauthorized preaching. For many Protestant churches, there was a great emphasis on the preacher being well educated and knowing the original languages. In the home, it was assumed that Protestant families would be literate, and efforts were made to ensure that this would be true. The Bible was read in daily family prayers and in private meditation. This was understood to be the norm of Protestant daily prayer.

Questions for Discussion

1. González emphasizes the effect that past advances in technology had on people's access to the Bible. What are some of the results of changes in media of communication that are, and will likely continue, influencing our contemporary reading and study of Scripture? How should the church respond to such changes?

2. During the period of the early church, the "rule of faith" served as a summary of the major beliefs of Christianity. Can you as individuals and/or as a group develop such a "rule of faith" for yourselves and for the church

today? What are the advantages and some of the problems of such an approach?

3. What versions (translations or paraphrases) of the Bible are used by members of your group? Discuss the characteristics, differences, strengths, and weaknesses of various versions.

4. The incursions of diverse Germanic peoples into the area of the western Roman Empire significantly affected the developing culture of Europe. The United States has always been a multicultural nation, but indisputably, the influence of groups such as African Americans, Asian Americans, and Hispanic Americans continues to become more conspicuous. What may be some of the influences of this cultural diversity on our understanding of the Bible?

Chapter 2

The Study of the Scripture in Early Methodism

Ben WITHERINGTON III

The Origins of Bible Study

THE YEAR WAS 1456 and in Mainz, Germany, a revolution had just occurred. Johannes Gutenberg had invented movable type and had printed a Latin Bible. It was the genesis of modern book making. When the first Bible rolled off Gutenberg's press, it is estimated there were only ninety Bibles in all of Europe. By the time that Columbus sailed for the new world in 1492, there were some 30,000. The importance of this invention can hardly be overestimated, and its connection to the Protestant Reformation can hardly be overstated. Indeed the Reformation that Luther sparked was fueled by his own intense study of the Scriptures, in particular the letters of Paul to the Galatians and Romans. Ordinary people studying the Bible is a by-product of the Protestant Reformation, and until the last fifty years or so, has primarily been the activity of Protestants.

If we press forward now to the early eighteenth century and look in on John Wesley, we discover a man who was thoroughly saturated in the Word of God. Anyone who has ever read Wesley's journal or any of his major works will know that the man spoke "Biblese." Not only could he quote large portions of Scripture, but he also was so saturated in Scripture that his very language reflected the diction of the Authorized Version, or as we would call it, the King James Version, and other versions used in *The Book of Common Prayer*.

Wesley repeatedly remarked that though he had read hundreds, perhaps thousands of books, nonetheless he was *homo unius libri*—a man of one book, the Good Book. It is no accident that the great revival of the eighteenth century was spearheaded by men like John and Charles Wesley and George Whitefield, men who were saturated in the Scriptures, and viewed all of life through the lens of Scripture. There would likely have been no Wesleyan revival, humanly speaking, if there had not first been persons like the Wesleys and Whitefield who had immersed themselves in the study of the Word and searched the Scriptures for guidance.

Consider also Francis Asbury in the late eighteenth and early nineteenth century riding thousands of miles up and down the east coast and into the Midwest of the United States, usually carrying with him only two things—his Bible and his journal. When Asbury sent out preachers in all directions the only thing he armed them with was the Word of God. He promised them no pay, but "grace here and glory hereafter." The benefits of the camp meetings would never have been lasting, and indeed in most places Methodist churches would never have been founded, without solid, biblically grounded preaching. But such preaching was only possible after intense study of God's Word. Such intense study of the Word by someone on the move was only possible as a result of the proliferation of copies of the Bible from the time of the Reformation onward.

I have in my possession a copy of Richard Watson's *The Life of the Rev. John Wesley, A.M.* printed in 1831 in New York. On the inside cover there is pasted the obituary of one

Miss Sarah Haughton, a long-time Methodist who died in 1834. It is a reminder of how precious and costly hardbound books were before the twentieth century. Sally Haughton, as she inscribed the book on the front flyleaf, in all likelihood had only a few books to her name and she probably kept important records in them, as many people still do. It is a reminder that most of the earliest Methodists had few of the tools we have for Bible study and those that they did have they used frequently and treated with great care. These early Methodists had no coffee table Bibles gathering dust. So how then did they study the Word and with what tools?

Not enough historical data is available for us to be able to say how typical Methodists studied the Bible. Instead, it will be necessary to concentrate on certain influential and better-known eighteenth- and nineteenth-century Methodist figures. Certainly ordinary Methodists followed the examples of those who led them in their societies, classes, and band meetings; and such local leaders followed the examples of their itinerant clergy. Our focus will be on John Wesley, Francis Asbury, and Richard Watson.[1] In this way we can begin to discern how the Word was handled and studied by the leaders of the movement.

Wesley on the Word

It has sometimes been thought that John Wesley was so focused on the Bible that he instilled in his converts a narrow-minded approach in which sources other than the Bible need not be considered. Nothing could be further from the truth. In his "Address to the Clergy" in 1756, Wesley says that the well-furnished minister must have "a capacity for reasoning with some closeness . . . a lively turn of thought . . . a good memory . . . a competent share of knowledge [including] Scripture in the original tongues, [plus] a knowledge of history . . . of sciences . . . metaphysics, . . .

41

natural philosophy . . . the history of Christian thought and devotion . . . [and] a knowledge of the world. . . ."[2] Where had Wesley gained such a broad vision of what needed to be known in order to study, much less to preach, God's Word?

The answer is surely found in his upbringing. Both of Wesley's parents were high church Anglicans, but both Samuel and Susanna Wesley were also the children of Puritan or Dissenter ministers. It was the Puritans especially among the Protestants who excelled in what we would call home schooling, not least because their children when they grew up would not be allowed to attend the major (Anglican sanctioned) universities at Oxford and Cambridge. Both parents contributed significantly to John Wesley's education, with Samuel providing John with some training in Greek and in Anglican worship, while Susanna concentrated on the array of other subjects. Most of the strictly religious training seems to have come from Susanna. She taught her children as much as six hours a day, from the time they had learned to talk. The very first thing they learned was to say the Lord's Prayer, which was to be recited at rising and at bedtime each day. Even before they could read, Susanna had taught John and the other children a short catechism, some portions of Scripture, and several prayers. The Bible was the Wesley children's very first reader, which they began to work through after they had learned their alphabet at age five. Every morning they read a psalm and a chapter of the Old Testament; in the evening, a psalm and a chapter of the New Testament. John maintained this practice throughout his life.

In December of 1711, when Samuel was away at the Anglican convocation, Bible study at the Epworth parsonage grew to include more than just the Wesley family. The assistant who had been left in charge of the parish was an unsatisfactory preacher. Typically, Susanna took matters into her own hands, enlarging family prayer time to include the reading of sermons and exhortations. As many as two hundred people sometimes packed the parsonage for these meetings, which attracted more attendance than the services in the parish church. Plainly, from his boyhood on, Wesley was trained to take very seriously the study of the Word, to apply himself wholeheartedly to it, and to use every pertinent resource available. Later in his own pilgrimage he would often return to some of the Puritan divines such as Matthew Henry or Richard Baxter, or the great German commentator Johannes Bengel, because his parents had provided such clear examples of the need for diligent Bible study with the aid of commentaries and sermons.

His heritage of the tradition of Puritan interpretation taught Wesley to take the Word as final authority on all matters it addressed and to take it in its literal or plain sense unless there were indications in the text that he ought to do otherwise. Wesley clearly recognized other, lesser authorities than Scripture such as reason, Christian tradition, and experience. These served as windows on the central truth of Scripture or vehicles through which that central truth could be expressed. He did not see reason, tradition, and experience as independent authorities; he never let them nullify the Scripture, although he did recognize that they should be used to apply the biblical Word appropriately. For Wesley, experience served basically to confirm the truth of Scripture inwardly and personally.

In analyzing Wesley's study of God's Word, it becomes clear that he held to a theory of double inspiration by the Holy Spirit first of the biblical author's and then of the believer's mind, guiding the interpretation of the text. Even more, the Spirit conveys and applies the truths of Scripture, leading the student of the Word into a clearer knowledge of the truth. Wesley believed that the essential function of Scripture was to provide knowledge of how one could be saved; this was its central theme. In Wesley's view, the Bible should not be seen as a compendium of all knowledge, but rather a collection of the historical, theological, and ethical truths one needs to know to be saved.

In January of 1754, Wesley decided that it was necessary for him to publish some "Notes upon the New Testament," which would provide something of a primer on how to study God's Word—what to look for in it and how to interpret it correctly. In his preface to that work he stressed that it is written for "plain unlettered" persons who understand only their mother tongue and yet love God's Word and wish to save their own souls.

Unlike many commentators of his age, he decided that he would offer only short guiding comments on the text. This was because Wesley believed, like many other post-Enlightenment Protestants, in both the clarity of Scripture and the essential trustworthiness of human reason. In short, he believed that with a clear translation and just a few helpful comments one who studied diligently could get at the "plain" meaning of the text:

> I have endeavoured to make the notes as short as possible, that the comment may not obscure or swallow up the text: and as plain as possible, in pursuance of my main design, to assist the unlearned reader: for this reason I have studiously avoided, not only all curious and critical inquiries, and all use of the learned languages, but all such methods of reasoning and modes of expression as people in common life are unacquainted with: for the same reason, as I rather endeavour to obviate than to propose and answer objections, so I purposely decline going deep into many difficulties, lest I should leave the ordinary reader behind me.[3]

Wesley does not dispute the value of learned detailed commentaries dealing with the original languages for educated clergy and scholars, but his point is that lay persons are not prepared for study at that level, and that the Bible must be allowed to be a book for all people. Wesley trusted the Word and the Spirit to do the work, while at the same time valuing the scholarly endeavor, especially for those who will be the major interpreters of the Word for lay persons.

A clue as to how Wesley himself studied the Word can be found in his preface to the *Standard Sermons*. Consider the following:

> Here then I am, far from the busy ways of men. I sit down alone: only God is here. In his presence I open, I read his book: for this end, to find the way to heaven. Is there a doubt concerning the meaning of what I read? Does anything appear dark or intricate? I lift up my heart to the Father of lights:—Lord, is it not thy word, "If any man lack wisdom, let him ask of God?" Thou "givest liberally, and upbraidest not." Thou has said, "If any be willing to do thy will, he shall know." I am willing to do, let me know thy will. I then search after and consider parallel passages of Scripture "comparing spiritual things with spiritual." I meditate thereon with all the attention and earnestness of which my mind is capable. If any doubt still remains, I consult those who are experienced in the things of God; and then the writings whereby, being dead, they yet speak. And what I thus learn, I teach.[4]

There are a variety of valuable points to be noted about this excerpt. First, Wesley suggests that one needs to get away from the distractions of work and busy places in order to properly study God's Word. It must be given one's undivided attention. Second, he believes that God in the person of the Holy Spirit is present with those studying the Word to illuminate them about its meaning. Third, the Bible is read with a particular spiritual end in mind—to understand the way of salvation, the way to heaven. This implies that it must be read with a searching heart, and with openness to receive personal benefit. One must own up to one's personal stake in such a study. This is no mere exercise in historical study or abstract contemplation. Rather one must be fully prepared to do what the text suggests once one discerns what God's will is. Fourth, if there is something obscure in the text, one follows a certain procedure to clarify matters: first, petition God in prayer for enlightment and understanding; second, compare parallel Scripture passages so that the clearer texts will make evident the meaning of the more obscure ones; third, meditate on the significance of these possible parallels, giving them full attention; fourth, consult experienced Christians for their guidance; and finally consult the writings of great Christians who have commented on the text.

This process is in many ways a very comprehensive description of how to go about doing a devotional study of the Bible and suggests that this is how Wesley would have his Methodists proceed. Wesley himself followed this procedure many times. If one visits Wesley's quarters within the New Room in Bristol, one can see the marks on the writing desk that is built into the window sill where Wesley has worn down the desk's rim with his books and the pressure of his hands writing and has also worn down the support underneath the desk with his foot from long hours of sitting, reading, studying, and writing. In this excerpt Wesley appears as the good Protestant interpreter he was, always believing that God and Scripture itself, not some human tradition, are the best guides to studying the Word; but in the end one must not refrain from using human resources as well to clarify matters. He is confident that while Scripture is clear, human minds are not always so, nor are they always in tune with what the Scripture intends to teach.[5]

We cannot leave our discussion of Wesley without saying something about how he saw the study of the Word as a means of grace. Wesley wanted, for himself and for his Methodists, the Word of God to dwell in the human heart richly, not to "make a short stay or an occasional visit, but take up its stated residence" and in "the largest measure, and with the greatest efficacy, so as to fill and govern the whole soul."[6] In Wesley's view, studying the Scripture can and often does lead to a person being transformed by God's grace. Not merely the Lord's Supper or baptism but also Bible study is seen as a means of grace. In Question 48 of the Large Minutes of the Methodist Conference, Wesley stressed the following definition of what he means by "search the Scriptures":

"(1) Reading: Constantly, some part of every day; regularly, all the Bible in order; carefully, with the Notes [e.g. his Notes upon the Old or New Testaments]; seriously, with prayer before and after; fruitfully, immediately practicising what you learn there. . . (2) Meditating: At set times? By any rule?"[7]

Wesley, like his Puritan forebears, did not want Christian converts who only knew the New Testament. Rather he wanted them to study the whole of the Bible diligently, prayerfully, carefully, precisely because so doing would lead to a blessing, to character formation, to growth in grace, to greater Christ-likeness. Prayer or the invoking of the Spirit before study was especially necessary because "Scripture can only be understood through the same Spirit whereby it was given. Our reading should likewise be closed with prayer, that what we read may be written on our hearts."[8]

The end result of Bible study done in the aforementioned manner is that one knows God, grasps God's will, and experiences God's love and grace. This in turn leads to the replication of God's character—both in inward and outward holiness, holiness of heart and life—in the student of the Word. One becomes what he or she admires in Scripture. We can understand, in the light of this view of Bible study and its potential results, why Wesley was so insistent in season and out that his Methodists become people of the Book.

Asbury: On the Road with the Word

By contrast with John Wesley, Francis Asbury was not well educated, was never an Oxford don, and never wrote any scholarly treatises. When pushed by Thomas Coke to help found a theological college for ministers in Maryland (called Cokesbury College), he went along with the plan; but when the school burned down shortly thereafter, Asbury said that he had simply wanted a lower level school not a college of this sort. On the other hand, since Asbury had indeed been a Methodist from an early age, in part through the influence of his mother, he had read many of the books recommended by Wesley in his Christian Library series to help improve his understanding of the Word.

Though Asbury could not match Wesley's acumen or scholarly expertise in the Bible, he was in no way less diligent in the way he studied the Word throughout his life. Consider the following two entries from his *Journal*:

> I purposed to rise at four o'clock, as often as I can, and spend two hours in prayer and meditation; two hours in reading, and one in recreating and conversation; and in the evening, to take my room at eight, pray and meditate an hour, and go to bed at nine o'clock: all this I purpose to do, when not traveling; but to rise at four o'clock every morning.

> This morning, I ended the reading my Bible through, in about four months. It is hard work for me to find the time for this; but all I read and write, I owe to early rising.[9]

As L. C. Rudolph stresses in his biography, Asbury knew the New Testament by memory, and he was an avid reader with a reading list including not only all the works recommended by Wesley (especially William Law and Richard Baxter whom Wesley admired) but also many others. He especially favored biographies of great Christians, sermons, and devotional works both ancient (such as Thomas á Kempis's *Imitation of Christ*) and from his own age.[10]

During the Revolutionary War when Asbury had to "locate" for a while in Delaware, he gave himself over to much reading and serious study of the Word. He even read many of the great Reformed divines such as Jonathan Edwards or John Bunyan but not nearly so often as he read and re-read Wesley's *Sermons, Notes*, and tracts. He even saw value in studying the Bible in several different languages, and did so in at least three, to get at the core of the meaning (*Journal*, March 16, 1778; April 7, 1778). In an age when there were not a multitude of English translations as there are today, Asbury was nonetheless modeling a form of Bible study that does not limit itself to one particular translation and always returns to the original languages when possible.

One of the interesting differences between Asbury and Wesley in their study and use of the Word is that Asbury was a little less reticent than Wesley to believe that Bible prophecies were being fulfilled in his own day and through his own ministry. He was a bit more given to allegorizing the text for the sake of contemporizing than Wesley usually was. In general, he approached the text with a bit less of a scholar's eye and a bit less insistence on the plain, literal meaning of the text. In this he was departing somewhat from some aspects of the Puritan Protestant heritage that so shaped Wesley. It should be noted that it was Asbury's habit for a long period of time to read the Book of Revelation every Sunday—one of his very favorite portions of Scripture for personal study. The *Journal* entry for May 10, 1778, says: "On the Lord's day I read the Revelation three times over, experienced great sweetness in my soul, both in reading and in family exercises." It was not just any sort of reading; it was reading, reflecting, and praying about matters. As L. C. Rudolph says, in the middle of a Bible study time he would schedule an hour for prayer because "the Devil will let us read always if we will not pray."[11]

When Asbury came to the American colonies, he felt it important that his preachers be very familiar with the *Standard Sermons* of Wesley and Wesley's *Notes upon the New Testament*. This meant that Asbury was a perpetrator of Wesley's approach to the study of the Scriptures. But, in the frontier conditions of the New World, there was little time, funds, or opportunity for Methodist preachers to carry more than the Bible and these two Wesley works with them. The old saying, "your sermons will only be as good as your library," could be applied in this case to their study of the Word. Just how drastic his preachers' needs for resources were can be seen from a letter written by Asbury on February 11, 1797, when he refers to the publication of the *Discipline* and says: "We [i.e., primarily Asbury and Coke] have written what will make about 100 printed pages, have bound our work with six or 700 printed scriptures. Our hearts, hands, heads, eyes, Bibles, and concordances have been employed." The motive for this exposition was that the Methodist preachers needed to be convinced on the basis of specific scriptural texts about various points in the *Discipline,* for they would see these two resources as the primary authorities in their churches and church work. It should be noted what resources Asbury himself says were used to produce this volume—Bibles, concordances, and a wholehearted application of all one's self and abilities and attention to the scriptural text.

A further clear indication of how difficult it would be for early Methodists including Methodist preachers, to have the resources to study the Word is shown by a variety of Asbury's letters about the fledgling Book Concern that was established to make Wesley's works and related spiritual resources available to Methodists in the New World. Ezekiel Cooper had been appointed editor and general book steward in 1799, succeeding John Dickins. The Methodist leaders in conference had approved statements about what books should be printed, but of course the problem was the lack of money. Asbury spoke not only of the urgency, but also the exigencies of the situation in a letter to Cooper dated January 8, 1799: "Conference voted, hit or miss, to carry on the work forthwith, and nominated several books to be printed immediately." But then he adds, "We feel our doubts concerning the printing of more books at present. We have some scruples upon our minds if it will be possible to carry on the work in Philadelphia in future. The collecting of money will be attended to by Brother Lee, with the greatest activity and punctuality."

Communications between Asbury and Cooper make clear that it was considered important to have resources for studying God's Word, but that finances were precarious. In a later letter to Cooper, dated January 7, 1801, Asbury referred to the printing of "our Scripture Catechism [which] is one of the best in the world, but it could be mended by you, and laid before the next Conference in the amendment." Asbury did not envision a purely theological catechism; instead he wrote, "I think now if you propound in your own language questions such as these, What is the duty of parents? What is the duty of husbands, wives, children, ministers, rulers, subjects, masters, servants? What is the duty of Christians one to another? and so on, and answer them wholly in Scripture, it would, in my view, be most excellent. We could enforce catechising if we had a complete guide." In Asbury's view, one of the major functions of studying Scripture and printing catechisms grounded in Scripture was wholly practical—to derive basic principles for daily Christian living.

Though he could not count on his Methodists to have vast resources for the study of the Word, Asbury could enforce a very regular period of time devoted to such study and reflection and he repeatedly did so. This was one function of the Methodist structures of the day that included the society meetings, the class meetings, the band meetings, and prayer meetings. Especially in the class and band meetings there would be times not only for questions and answers about one's weekly progress in the Christian life, but also time for the study of and reflection on the Word, and an exhortation based on it.[12]

There were a variety of reasons why Asbury, who even as

a child had earned the title "Methodist parson" because of his piety and burying his nose in the Bible, thought the study of God's Word was crucial. In a letter written to his mother and dated June 28, 1799, we get a glimpse of one of these reasons: "The coming of Christ is near, even at the door, when he will establish his kingdom. He is now sweeping the earth, to plant it with righteousness and true holiness. My eyes are weak enough, even with glasses. When I was a child, and would pry into the Bible by twinkling firelight, you used to say, 'Frank, you will spoil your eyes.' At that time, I sought the historical letter. I knew not the hidden pure light and life." The first and last comments from this entry are of special interest. Bible study was crucial if one wanted to be prepared for Christ's return, possibly in the near future.[13] Yet not just any sort of Bible study would avail for such preparation. One needed to learn to read the Bible so as to discern its spiritual message and purposes, not simply because of its historical interest or vivid stories.

In another very interesting letter to Ezekiel Cooper, dated December 31, 1801, Asbury indicated that he had been pushing for certain resources to be published including the Methodist hymnbook. He stressed that printing and reprinting of key portions of the works of Wesley and Joseph Fletcher are crucial—"As a friend, I would advise you . . . to keep close to Fletcher's and Wesley's most excellent parts." Such works were the staple diet of the early Methodists and gave them their theological and ethical guidance for how to read the Bible.

A few other clues about Asbury's study and use of the Bible can be gleaned from his abbreviated sermon notes that occur from time to time in his *Journal*. For example, in the *Journal* entry for December 8, 1794, he spoke of addressing an unresponsive crowd: "I opened the Bible on [Jeremiah 14:10]. Let any one read it as an awful portion; it may be it is as true to these people as it was to Israel." What Asbury was suggesting is that by analogy, the situation of Israel and

God's people in his day could be similar enough that the exhortation to the one could serve as an exhortation to the other. This was based on an understanding that Scripture reveals that there is a pattern to: God's dealings with his people; the behavior of God's people; and the way God responds to their unresponsiveness. Israel and its behavior are seen as a type of, and a lesson for, every generation of believers.

Even more interesting is the *Journal* entry for Sunday, December 14, 1800. Asbury was preaching on Matthew 17:5 but was struck by the close parallel to the wording of what God said to Jesus at his baptism (Matthew 3:17 and parallel passages). He then proceeded to unpack each key term in the sentence spoken by God—"This is my Son in whom I am well pleased":

> First the Divine Father acknowledged the sacred and mysterious union—"This is my beloved Son": a relation infinitely above that of angels, of Adam in his primeval standing, and the souls of any regenerated, sanctified, or glorified soul, on earth or in heaven—co-equal, co-eternal, and co-essential with the Father. "Well-pleased!"—that is, in the whole of man's redemption by this "beloved Son": "well-pleased"—in his preaching, living, dying—in every part of his official character. "Hear ye him"—Mark and Luke have omitted *ye*. Secondly the particular characters who should hear him in his word, Spirit, and operations. His ministers should hear him—this was designed in the text, by *ye*: hear him all his sanctified souls; hear him all who are justified; hear him all ye seekers; hear him all ye sinners—hear his awful warnings: all ye backsliders, hear him as Peter heard him, and repent, and turn to him; hear him ye apostates, as Judas, and despair.[14]

What we should gather from this is that Asbury believed that any biblical text should be closely scrutinized and milked for all its worth. It should be compared to other similarly worded texts, and the differences should also be taken into account. In other words, attention must be given to the text in its literary context and in depth.

A good example of the way Asbury, through diligent study and application, could allegorize a text and so make it more relevant to his audience, can be seen in his comments on Romans 13:12 ("The night is far spent"—meant metaphorically of the eschatological time Paul was living in.) These comments appear in the *Journal* entry for September 3, 1815. First he deals with the analogy as he finds it (dealing first with natural then with spiritual darkness), next he allegorizes:

> What constitutes the natural *night*? Absence of light, ignorance, insecurity, uncertainty. The Gospel watchman crieth the hours. The Scripture night; from Adam to Moses. The patriarchal stars and those who preceded them as dim lights, Adam, Abel, Enoch, Noah, Abraham. The moon-light of the law, the Sabbaths, the sacrifices. But this night was about to pass away, although darker just before the dawn of the Gospel day; and it is thus in nature. . . . And would not some of our great men, if they dared, bring a night of infidelity on this land? Who sees them in regular attendance on the house of God? "Let us cast off the works of darkness." Let us not sin in practice. Let us cast off evil tempers, desires, and affections.[15]

Asbury's diligence in Bible study, his learning of the Word, his attendance on it both morning and evening, his praying during Bible study for illumination, his belief that he was receiving not merely information but revelation through the Spirit's illumination of the text, his attention to context and parallels both textual and experiential, both ancient and modern, are all the traits of the serious Bible student of his day. While we might not want to encourage the sort of allegorizing of the text in which he occasionally engages, we have to admire his diligence in the attempt to apply the text to his audience and to see the similarities in their situations and that of the earlier generations of God's people.

Asbury's approach to the text does not differ markedly from Wesley's except in some of the small ways we have mentioned. Throughout, he exudes that notable Protestant confidence that the Bible is clear in its meaning, that it is its own best interpreter, and that in any event it should be read in light of its great theme (the so-called *analogia fidei*)—God's plan of salvation to create a redeemed people.[16]

Richard Watson

There can be little doubt about the importance and influence of Richard Watson for American Methodism. His *Theological Institutes* were the textbook of theology in the nineteenth century for Methodist preachers, in addition to Wesley's *Notes* and *Sermons,* and were a required part of the course of studies. Watson's life of John Wesley was the standard biography that Methodists read. Much was learned by early Methodists from Watson about how to read and study the Bible. I wish here to gather some insights from his own sermons, which best help us to see how he approaches and handles the text. It needs to be kept in mind that Watson, like Wesley, was indeed a scholar and, unlike Asbury, he did not spend most of his time on long journeys on horseback. Nor was he burdened with the huge administrative load of running a fledgling church that was spread out over hundreds of miles. Watson remained in England and made his contributions mainly from the study and the pulpit. A careful Protestant scholar of his day, he was closer to Wesley than Asbury in his skill and ability to handle the original languages in which Scripture was written. He was the younger contemporary of Asbury and lived to see the Methodist connection well established in the United Kingdom in the first decades of the nineteenth century. Watson had an especial concern for missions, including overseas, and helped found many of the Methodist missions societies in England. Indeed, the first sermon we will examine was preached in Albion Street Chapel, Leeds, at the formation of the Methodist Missionary Society there on October 6, 1813.

Watson was as keen as Asbury, if not keener, on the prophetic portions of the Scriptures, but unlike Asbury he did not think them specific enough to allow for date or place setting and the like. The text from which he preached on the aforementioned occasion was Ezekiel 37:9—the familiar dry bones vision. Watson offered this warning near the beginning of the sermon:

> We are not, however, to suppose that our view of the future, even after the most attentive study of the prophetical books will be perfectly distinct and satisfactory. There is a moral necessity that prophecy should be surrounded with a certain haze and indistinctness. Man is to be the instrument of executing the decrees of Heaven; and it is the principle of the Divine government to offer no violence to his moral agency, and a peculiar glory of infinite wisdom to accomplish its purposes by his free volitions. It seems, therefore to be a mistake in many persons to expect to ascertain the exact times and manner in which the predictions of Heaven will be accomplished. Time is the grand expounder of prophecy; and as far as relates to particulars, perhaps time alone. The value of prophecy is not, however, on this account, diminished. In this partial form it fully answers the design of God, by supporting the confidence of good men in the ultimate triumphs of their religion, in quickening their exertions, and [in] relieving their anxieties.[17]

This is a most intriguing statement, and it becomes even more so when Watson goes on to say that if "the prediction [of Ezekiel] referred at all to the restoration of the Jews from the Babylonian captivity, it could only be in a very low sense. The terms in which it is expressed plainly indicate an event more glorious in its accomplishment, more permanent in its effects, and more spiritual in nature. It connects itself with the glory of the latter day."[18] Yet remarkably, what Watson is really interested in is using this text as a figure or allegory of the current spiritual death of the largely heathen world in which he lived, and of what he calls its "mystical" resurrection. Yet before we dismiss Watson as just another allegorizer, it is in order to note that Ezekiel himself seems to have had in mind not the literal resurrection of a dead Israelite army, but rather the spiritual resurrection of God's people, in part by means of their return to Jerusalem and Judea. In short, Watson's exposition would seem to be closer to the original intent of the text in taking the picture as primarily figurative in character, than those who insisted on taking it literally.

What do we learn here about early Methodist study of the prophetic portions of the Bible? First, we learn that they were prepared to reckon with a certain indeterminancy or opaqueness to the prophetic texts in regard to particulars. The caution about date setting and the like is well taken and as Watson suggests, such a practice would be a violation of the more general character of the prophecy. Second, we learn that in the first place these prophecies were meant for Israel, even though Watson assigns this reading of the text to its "low sense." He was convinced there is a spiritual or mystical sense to the text that still has much relevance even for a very different age and audience. In his view this was always a part of the meaning of the text; it is not something we read into it, and in fact it requires even now the proper spiritual discernment to recognize this meaning in the text. Last, we cannot overlook the stress placed by Watson on the role God's people have in fulfilling God's prophecies. Watson had no doubt that these are true; oracles from God, and oracles are intended to come true; but he believed that to some real extent their fulfillment depends on our cooperation with God's plan, and in this case the application is not far to see for his own audience: unless they begin diligently supporting the mission society's work, the world will remain a place of dry bones and spiritual death.

Watson's sermon then proceeds to discuss the many slain by sin, lying under God's curse on sin. Going beyond even Ezekiel's figurative character he says things like—" 'they were unburied:' the destructive effects of sin, the sad ravages of death, lay exposed and open to the sun. . . . This representation strongly marks the dreadful maturity of sin among apostate nations, and the absence of all those checks which in countries better instructed restrain evils which are not wholly cured."[19]

Again, of course, there is some continuity with Ezekiel's exposition here. However, Ezekiel has a particular nation in mind, Israel, rather than nations in general who were at odds with God, and Ezekiel does not go so far as to spell out what various aspects of the picture might represent, as does Watson. Such an exposition does indeed lead and lend itself to allegorizing the text, and, in fact, Watson was to go on further to say things like the dryness of the bones represents the hopelessness of the condition of those being described. In this fashion, prophecy was brought to bear in a spiritual way on Watson's own audience, though one may suspect that the original prophet would have been surprised by some aspects of this exposition and application and in agreement with other aspects of it.

It is fitting to close the discussion of this sermon and what it tells us about Watson's approach to studying prophetic texts by a quotation from another sermon: "The prophets of the Old Testament not only expressed themselves in the elevated language of figure and poetry, but in many instances used a symbolic action to convey the messages they were commissioned to deliver to men. . . . In their case the Holy Spirit made use of a strong oriental imagination to convey his revelations; and this faculty was not less instructive in their hearers than in themselves."[20] Notice how Watson like Wesley insisted on the notion of double inspiration or illumination—of both the scriptural author and the Christian reader—and further, notice how Watson stressed that the Old Testament prophecies were in themselves figurative and poetic and, therefore, gave license to interpret them in accord with that fact. A crude literalism would miss the larger point of such prophetic texts in Watson's view.

It was normal practice among eighteenth- and nineteenth-century Protestant students of the Bible to read the historical portions of the Old Testament in typological fashion, seeing persons as precursors and foreshadowings of Christ or other New Testament persons. For instance, Watson says about Isaac that he was "not only a type of Christ, but also of the character and privileges of the Church of Christ. He alone was made the heir of his father's substance; and the profane son of the bond woman was cast out. In like manner, none are the heirs of God but those who are of the true spiritual seed; none enjoy the privileges of the Church but those who are holy and harmless; profane mockers and workers of iniquity have no part in the kingdom of God and of Christ."[21]

Lest we too quickly accuse Watson of being guilty of anachronism, it must be remembered that the authors of the New Testament encourage this very sort of reading of the historical portions of the Old. For example, in 1 Corinthians 10, Paul quite clearly portrays the Israelites as a type of the Corinthians themselves to warn them that they too, if they continue to behave as they were doing, might likewise "perish in the desert." Typology exegesis of the Old Testament assumes that God acts in similar fashion throughout all generations of God's people, and furthermore that God's people seem always to get themselves in the same kinds of predicaments, and that therefore analogies are appropriate.

It must be made clear that one of the abiding principles of Bible study for Wesley, Asbury, and Watson was that the Bible should be read not merely front to back, but even more importantly back to front. By this I mean that the Old Testament must be read in the light of Christ and the Christian dispensation, looking for promise and fulfillment, prediction and completion, antetype and type, and the like. Such a principle clearly guided the study and exposition of Watson.

It is, however, interesting to notice the difference in the way Watson approached Old Testament historical narrative from the way he approached its prophecy. Whereas prophecy should often be seen as figurative and poetic in character, "the biography of the Scriptures is written in a style peculiar to itself. Here is no laboured description, no tedious narration; all is free, artless, and simple. Yet the sacred writers, by a single stroke of the pen, give us a more correct view of the characters they describe than could possibly be conveyed by the labour of volumes. . . ."[22] In short, the historical portions can be read rather straightforwardly and one can do character studies or studies of character traits that are relevant to Christian growth and maturation.

It was Watson's profound conviction that the Word and its truths required meditation to really plumb the depths. "Meditation is to all these truths, which shine around us in their meridian splendour, what the opened eye is to the light; it admits them into the understanding as objects of knowledge, and it applies them as the spring and rule of practice. For neither the extent of them, as doctrines, can be seen, nor the advantages of them, as promises, be enjoyed, until they become the subjects of serious reflection and habitual devotion."[23] In other words, even though the narrative portions of the Word are clear enough, their larger significance for our own lives requires meditation and contemplation on these great verities. It allows us not only to know the Word and the world better but also to know ourselves better and how we fit into the grand scheme of things. Such meditation promotes the ultimate aim and end of Bible study, which is not mere knowledge but holiness, Christlikeness. We are to become like the One we admire and seek in Scripture. But meditation also leads to closer union with the One who inspired the Scripture. Watson puts it this way: "Would you then, my brethren, enjoy the highest privilege of human beings,—to walk and talk with God as a man with his friend, nay, to be 'joined to the Lord and become one spirit with him,'—retire . . . to meditate; keep your appointments with God sacred: he will not fail to meet you. 'Behold, I stand at the door and knock: if any man hear my voice, and open the door, I will come in to him, and will sup with him, and he with me.' "[24] In Watson's view, it is not merely the Word one encounters in such contemplative reflection on Scripture, but the Word Incarnate.

In his sermon entitled "The Oracles of God," Watson spoke of both the character of the Word and the appropriate reverence required in one's approach to it. Watson was convinced that God is speaking to us in all parts of the Bible. It may all be called the oracles of God, and not just any kind of oracles, but living ones:

> It is this which constitutes the grand peculiarity of the word of God. It is a word with which the Spirit of God wonderfully works; and which he renders living. No other book has this peculiarity. Show me one which all the wicked fear; which lays a secret dread upon the boldest; which cuts deep into the conscience, and rouses salutary fears; which comforts and supports; and while its blessed truths quiver on the lips of the dying, disarms death of its sting. Show me such a book, and you show me the Bible. In all the crowded libraries of the world you can find no other that possesses such power.[25]

Maximum benefit then accrues to those who approach the Bible in the manner in which Moses approached the burning bush—with respect, with reverence, with anticipation. "With the oracles of God the Author is present, whether you read or hear; and you have 'thoughts that' truly 'breathe, and words that burn.' You cannot avoid this power. It will make the word either 'a savour of life unto life or a savour of death unto death.' "[26] In other words, in Watson's view, picking up the Bible is like picking up a one-thousand–volt electrical cable—it requires handling with care, prayer, and respect.

Watson means to stress that while not everything we are curious about finds an answer in Scripture, everything we need for salvation is certainly contained there. He believes that the Bible contains the fulness of truth about this matter and so "the Bible is ever new."[27] Bible study can never exhaust its meaning or fail to reward the diligent seeker after truth.

Yet precisely because the Bible contains the living oracles of God, "it is a sin of no ordinary magnitude to pervert their meaning. Take heed how you read and hear. The Bible contains that 'truth which is according to godliness.' ... To pervert these holy oracles, so as to give encouragement to impiety, is to incur a responsibility at which the stoutest heart may justly tremble. . . . It is [also] a great sin to restrain the Scriptures. . . . Teach these oracles to your children and servants, and assist in circulating them to the ends of the earth."[28]

Were we to explore Watson's works at greater length, we would find similar remarks in other texts as well. Watson, like Wesley and Asbury, did not approach Bible study by the method of historical criticism that became popular in the nineteenth century. Yet they were not unaware of the difficulties, textual and otherwise, of the Bible. It was their view however that one should not concentrate on such matters. This is not to say that they were only interested in the devotional or spiritual reading of the text. Indeed, all three of these early Methodists would have been adamant about the historical substance and claims of the Scripture and about the need for studying the Word in its literary and historical context. Yet all of them shared a confidence that in regard to what it intends to teach, the Bible is clear and fully trustworthy in conveying the truth.

Watson's approach to Bible study was in various regards

more systematic than that of Asbury. He clearly operated with differing exegetical principles and approaches for the differing types of Scripture, such as prophecy, narrative, and Wisdom Literature.[29] He viewed both prophecy and Wisdom Literature as largely figurative and poetic in character. His exhortations to devote oneself wholeheartedly to the study of the Scriptures simply echo those of Wesley and Asbury and need not be repeated here. What does need to be stressed is the way Watson modeled in-depth study of the Word for a whole century of American Methodists, especially Methodist preachers. More careful attention to how he, and Wesley and Asbury, "rightly explained the word of truth" would repay a great deal of further study.

Stewards of the Living Word

In many ways Wesley established a rather clear pattern for profitable Bible study by both what he did and what he said in his most widely circulated works the *Sermons* and the *Notes upon the New Testament*. It will do well to reiterate what he said here. First, one needs to get away from the distractions of work and busy places in order properly to study God's Word. It must be given one's undivided attention. Second, God in the person of the Holy Spirit is present with those studying the Word to illuminate them about its meaning.   Third, the Bible is read with a particular spiritual end in mind—to understand the way of salvation, the way to heaven. This implies that it must be read with a searching heart, and with openness to receive personal benefit. One must own up to one's personal stake in such a study. This is no mere exercise in historical study or abstract contemplation. Rather one must be fully prepared to do what the text suggests once one discerns what God's will is. Fourth, if there is something obscure in the text one follows a certain procedure to clarify matters: first, petition God in prayer for enlightenment and understanding; second, compare parallel Scripture passages so that the clearer texts will make evident the meaning of the more obscure ones; third, meditate on the significance of these possible parallels, giving them full attention; fourth, consult experienced Christians for their guidance; and finally consult the writings of great Christians who have commented on the text. This is in many ways a very comprehensive description of how to go about doing a devotional study of the Bible; this is how Wesley would have his Methodists proceed.

From a close examination of Asbury's and Watson's works, we garner some further clues. One of these is about the value and validity of distinguishing between the surface meaning of a text and its larger spiritual import. Sometimes, it is true, this led both Asbury and Watson into allegorizing a nonallegorical text, but normally it was done in a spirit that was in accord with the general tenor or gist of the text. The plain sense of the text guided the more metaphorical expansions on it. We also saw ample evidence that prayer, meditation, contemplation, and a seeking of union with God were advocated as essential accompanying practices to make Bible study truly profitable. Watson adds a needed stress on paying attention to the different genre of literature in the Bible and interpreting them appropriately.

It also needs to be noted that all these remarks are intended for those who are already Christians. Neither Wesley, nor Asbury, nor Watson is talking about Bible study for just anyone. This becomes especially clear in their comments about double inspiration in the Word and in the believing reader. The exhortations to diligent, daily, devotional study of the Word assume such an audience.

Finally, we may conclude this discussion with the exhortation and maxim Wesley himself passed along to his Methodists as a most salutary word and guide to Bible study: "Apply the whole of the text to yourself; apply the whole of yourself to the text." Our Methodist forebears would have us all be good stewards of the mysteries of God, but this can only happen if we immerse ourselves in the study of the Bible.

Questions for Discussion

1. Witherington points out that for Wesley and Asbury, and many other early Methodists, their active lives of ministry made it difficult to find time for Bible study. Compare and contrast the problem of time management that Christians deal with today. What can be learned from Wesley and Asbury about how we, like them, can "make room" in our lives for personal and corporate attention to Scripture?

2. What did Wesley mean when he referred to himself as "a man of one book"? What clues can we gain from Wesley that will make our biblical study and interpretation more meaningful?

3. For many United Methodists, the prophetic books of the Old Testament are quite confusing. What can Watson's sermon teach us about understanding biblical prophecy?

4. We are fortunate to have readily accessible to us, not only the "tools" for biblical study that these three early Methodist leaders used, but also many others. What are some of these tools, and how can they help us? Look at catalogues from Cokesbury Bookstores and Discipleship Resources and identify some resources that you could encourage your church to make available or perhaps purchase for your own use.

Chapter 3

A Contemporary Approach: Interpreting the Bible in Historical Context

C. Everett TILSON

THE KEY WORD in this title is *contemporary,* for most contemporary interpreters of the Bible share this common denominator: they believe that, before the Bible can facilitate our experience of the divine/human dialogue, we must pay as close attention to the historical context of its writers as we give to the historical context of its readers. For them, and for me, the nouns *history* and *context*—and, by the same token, the adjectives *historical* and *contextual*—can be treated as virtual synonyms. This presentation is a plea to take with utmost seriousness the traditional description of biblical/Christian faith as a historical religion.

While few interpreters of the Bible would dispute its characterization as the expression of a historical religion, many of them have done less than justice to its historical character. Gordon Kaufman laments this failure in his *Systematic Theology*, a book in which he promised to take the historical character of biblical/Christian faith not just with utmost seriousness, but with absolute seriousness: "Although much is said about the significance of the fact that Christianity is a 'historical religion,' seldom," he declares, "is the full import of these words carried . . . into every crevice and corner of the theological interpretation of faith. Moreover," he adds, "the relationship between (salvation history) . . . and the ordinary, workaday . . . history . . . of our lives remains almost entirely unspecified. So despite its interest in 'history' the Christian faith appears to many . . . to be . . . completely irrelevant to the only history . . . they know."[1]

Kaufman fails to make good on his promise to take the "historical character" of our (biblical/Christian) faith with absolute seriousness. Yet there is no denying his charge that we have paid too little attention to the connection between salvation history and ordinary history. From every age, land, and tongue, Christians have provided him with quotable quotes with which to document his indictment. Many such persons, while quite ready to describe biblical/Christian faith as a historical religion, have nevertheless looked with suspicion on the effort to trace its history. And sometimes, even while insisting on the humanity of the prophets and apostles and Jesus, they have deplored all efforts to reconstruct their self-understanding. In short, despite their designation of biblical/Christian faith as a genuinely historical religion, they have proceeded to interpret it as a historical religion without regard for its historical context.

Though disappointed, I was not really surprised by Kaufman's inability to make biblical/Christian faith completely relevant to the only history which we human beings know. Given the long history of interpreting the Bible as if it had originated outside history, he would have surprised me only if he had fully succeeded in this undertaking.

While Kaufman did not fully accomplish his task, we contemporaries of his nevertheless accept his goal—to take the historical character of biblical/Christian faith with utmost or absolute seriousness—as our point of departure for interpreting the Bible. Below I shall briefly delineate the major requirements of this approach to biblical interpretation in terms of three propositions. However, before doing so, I should alert you to the reason behind my frequent substitution of "the

Word of God" for the Bible in the following pages. It is not because I view the Bible as a compilation of the literal words of God to humanity. Quite the contrary, it is because *word* is the vehicle of communication between two parties, the speaker and the hearer, each of whom brings their own special understanding of its meaning. This is not to deny the possibility of God serving as the speaker in such an encounter, but it is to acknowledge the fact that "the word" comes to us in the language not of God but of human beings. Hence the propositions that follow may be regarded as the defining requirements for a contemporary interpretation of the Bible:

First, the Word of God must not be interpreted without regard for its total history, because it cannot adequately be interpreted any other way.

Second, no part of human life or the world can any more be omitted from the context of the Word of God than a part of human life or the world can be excluded from the sovereignty of God. In developing this proposition, I shall single out commercial and political activity for special consideration. A religion stripped of all concern for commercial and political activity has lost its relevance; such a brand of religion has no biblical pedigree. Certainly its spokesperson cannot claim kinship with the Old Testament prophets. And the claim of such a person to be an updated model of a New Testament evangelist would be equally suspect. Even in the Book of Revelation where concern for the first heaven and earth yields center stage to the new heaven and earth, at least as great emphasis falls on present actualities as on future possibilities. What distinguishes the members of this second community from those of the first is not that their dwelling place transcends space and time. Neither is it the absence of concern for the patterns of social organization normally associated with economics and politics. Quite the contrary, it may be described as an "infinite qualitative distinction" that has to do, as Paul Minear has so aptly put it, with "God-relatedness."[2] Hence the crucial question for them is not *whether* they shall engage in commercial and political undertakings but *how*. Instead of debating the question—what has the new Jerusalem to do with Capitol Hill or Wall Street?—they will be at work trying to bridge the gap between the kingdom of God and the world of politics and economics.

And third, granted a dynamic understanding of history, we dare not write the future of the Word of God on the basis of its past.

The Inseparable Connection Between the Word of God and Its History

The Word of God must not be interpreted without regard for it total history, because it cannot adequately be interpreted any other way. When I use the word *total* in this connection, I mean that we must refuse to settle for anything less than *all* of history. Thus construed, the history of the Word of God embraces every important moment and event in the production and transmission of the Bible and its faith. Therefore, when I single out from this long history the three stages, respectively, of revelation, canonization, and interpretation for special consideration, I do not do so because it is only at these points that we are given a clue to the origin and meaning of the Word of God. Quite the contrary, I call them to our attention because they mirror the inescapable involvement of the Word of God in the life and language and experience of humankind. They illustrate what happens to the Word of God at every stage in its history by spotlighting the human elements at work in the most crucial stages of its history.

Revelation

The readiness of Israel's prophets to describe God's revelation to them as "the word of the Lord" has often been taken as proof of the divine authorship of their utterances and, hence, the ground for removal of the issues with which they dealt from the arena of public debate. Yet these same prophets, in instance after instance, followed up their invitation to listen for the Lord's word with the announcement of utterly conflicting demands in the Lord's name. Its divine origin notwithstanding, "the word" clothed itself in the prophets' own language, and it addressed issues familiar alike to the prophets and to their contemporaries. When studied against their historical background, one can no longer doubt that the deliverances of the prophets in the name of the Lord came to Israel in the words of the prophets. In fact, one can scarcely avoid wondering whether Israel, when it listened to the words of the prophets, also heard "the word of the Lord."

Therefore, if one speaks of God "writing" the Bible, that person is obviously speaking metaphorically. It would be blasphemous to think of God taking pen in hand and writing as a scribe writes. Just as obviously, it would be blasphemous, when speaking of God uttering words as a prophet speaks, to suppose one is not likewise speaking metaphorically. What is written or spoken in God's name may indeed come from firsthand encounter with God, but it is a human being and not God who does the reporting.

A prophet or apostle may well have thought he had settled the question of God's will by his proclamation of "the word of the Lord." But that proclamation, even though its focal concern may have been God's before it became that of God's spokesperson, did not cease to be human because it had its inspiration in God. In other words, the prophet's proclamation to Israel was truly *the prophet's* proclamation to Israel. By the same token, the "word of the Lord," if indeed that was what the prophet proclaimed, comes to us in the words not of the Lord but of the prophet. For as the Lord's thoughts are not as our thoughts, so the "Word of God" must never be equated with human words, not even if that person be a prophet or an apostle. Even God's spokespersons still spoke as human beings and not as God.

In view of this fact, we need to be clear about what it is we are saying when we speak of revelation as God's communication to human beings. It is not that God, in dialogue with us human beings, ceases to be God. It is that we, in dialogue with God, do not cease to be human. Similarly, when we describe God's address to us in terms of human speech, that is not because God speaks with the tongue and words of a human being. Rather, it is because we, even when receiving and reporting a revelation from God, hear with the ears, speak with the tongues, and understand with the minds of human beings.

Canonization

Both the Jewish and Christian communities produced numerous religious writings, some of which espoused teachings that were in conflict with those of other highly regarded writings. Fearful that this diversity, if allowed to go unchecked, might fragment their communities, the leaders of both communities took steps to define the boundaries of their faith. They drew up lists of the writings that could be regarded as authoritative for deducing the rules of faith and conduct. They called such a list a *canon*, a term derived from the Greek word meaning "instrument of measure."

While the Jewish and Christian communities each produced canons of sacred writings in their effort to stabilize the beliefs and conduct of their members, neither wholly succeeded in this undertaking. Unable to agree on just which books should be granted canonical status, they each produced not *a* canon but canons of sacred writings. In each community certain factors were at work that kept some of its members from accepting the Bible of others of its members. While the Jews inside Palestine and the Jews outside

Palestine both regarded their Bible as the bearer of God's Word, their Bibles were not the same. Just as human factors affected the revelation of the Word of God, they also affected the canonization of the Word of God.

The impact of history on the Word of God at the canonizing stage can easily be demonstrated. I would have only, as a typical Protestant, to declare that the Bible is the Word of God in the company of a group of typical Catholics or practicing Jews. Conceding the truth of my affirmation, they would assume that I was talking not only about *the* Bible, but about *their* Bible. Yet that would not be the case at all. For just as the Protestant Bible contains books that do not appear in the Jewish Bible, the Catholic Bible contains books absent from the Protestant Bible. So the obvious question arises: About whose Bible are we talking?

Consideration of this issue takes us directly into the historical situation behind the separation, first, of Christianity from Judaism and, next, of Protestant from Catholic Christianity. We cannot carry this pursuit very far without learning that the Bible, in addition to being "the Word of God," is also a monument to major ecclesiastical disputes. It took shape, in each instance, around the disputed claims of competing parties in the throes of vigorous conflict. So the Bible is a monument forged by human hands on the anvil of historical turmoil and struggle.

Because of this fact, we can scarcely understand *our* Bible without studying it against the background of its differentiation from the Bibles of others. Despite its obvious differences from other books, to which we must take care to do justice, we must likewise take care to do justice to its quite obvious similarities to other books. Since it, like other books, took shape in response to the needs of a particular people at a definite place and a specific time in a concrete situation, we must make every effort to reconstruct the special circumstances of its very special history. Anyone who knows the story of the canon, whether yours or mine, also knows that its framers were as much driven by the desire to solve the problems of human beings as they were moved by concern for the preservation of the Word of God. This is not to deny their overriding concern for the Word of God as the basis of their claim to be God's people, but it is to assert that their interest in religious authority was secondary to their concern for the needs of their community.

"The Royal Castle of the Word," Protestantism's house of refuge from the whims of tradition, has come under siege. The stones in its foundation have begun to shift, and already it is safe to say that its days as a secure ecclesiastical fortress are numbered. But this change, unlike that which claimed the Jewish Temple, will be an inside job. In fact, it has been in process ever since the beginning of biblical criticism, and most of its participants have been recruited from the ranks of former refugees.

This is not to question the motives of the practitioners of biblical criticism, as if, from their first timid inquiries concerning the sources of biblical literature, they could have foreseen the conclusions to which contemporary scholars would come from their study of the growth and development of the Bible. Or as if they could have foreseen that their insistence on the functional character of the individual books of the Bible would later be applied to the ecclesiastical decisions that gave us, in turn, the Jewish Bible, the Catholic Bible, and the Protestant Bible! Or as if they could have foreseen that their efforts would produce this ironic consequence: that, instead of establishing the priority of the Scripture over tradition and the Bible over the church, they would compel us to recognize the process of canonization itself as a by-product of the believing communities' quest for identity!

Each of these communities construed its canon, though different from the canons of the other communities, as the rule for its faith and life and, therefore, as a ground for distinguishing it from these other communities. In light of this fact, we can no longer accept at face value the claim of Protestant Christians that for them, unlike Catholics for whom the church is the primary authority, the Bible is the primary authority. For just as there was a Catholic church before there was a Catholic Bible, there was a Protestant church before there was a Protestant Bible. Moreover, just as it was a church decision that won for the Apocrypha a place in the Catholic Bible, it was a church decision that denied it a place in the Protestant Bible.

Canonical studies have done much to restore the respect of us Protestants for tradition and community. Although we can only draw this conclusion from the vantage point of a century and a half of hindsight, all the various types of biblical criticism may now be seen as successive contributors to this development. The source critics questions of when, where, why, under what circumstances, and to whom made it perfectly clear that the community played an important role in the production of the Scripture. The form critics helped to clarify this role by demonstrating the fact that the Scripture served a social function. The tradition critics established the fact that the Scripture, just as it was shaped to meet community needs, could also be revised to meet community needs. And the canonical critics have shown us that the standard for fixing the limits of the Bible—whether Jewish, Catholic or Protestant—were themselves products of the community's effort to determine just who it was and what it should be and do.

That the Israelites never ceased to adapt what they adopted is nowhere more clearly indicated than in Judaism's separation of the Book of Joshua from the first five books of the Old Testament (called the Torah by Jews). Although Israel's story was so remarkably elastic that it could be compressed into a single verse (1 Samuel 12:8) or expanded into hundreds of verses (Ecclesiasticus/Sirach 44–50), apparently its oldest versions (Exodus 15; Deuteronomy 26:5-9; Joshua 24:2-14; Psalms 105; 106; 135; 136) boasted at least three indispensable elements: the Exodus from Egypt, the sojourn in the wilderness, and the occupation of the land of Palestine. Surely it is no accident that the concluding episode in the Book of Joshua has its setting in Shechem, the site of Abraham's initial settlement in Canaan. By this ending the editors responsible for joining together the first six books of the Bible were seeking, as Professor James A. Sanders reminds us, to make this very important point: "the conquest of Canaan culminated in the very place Abraham first settled; the promise of land, which was made to Abraham at Shechem, was symbolically fulfilled at Shechem."[3] Since the story of Israel's national origins could not have been legitimated without the record of the conquest, we can be confident that "at one point the Torah concluded with the book of Joshua. In fact, it is rather shocking," declares Sanders, "that the Torah, as is, does not include the conquest of Canaan."[4]

Yet Joshua ceased to be a part of the Torah, and the reasons are as clear as the events of the sixth century B.C. were traumatic for the Jewish exiles in Babylonian captivity. Bereft of land, temple, and country, they were left with no important nationalistic symbols around which they could organize their self-understanding as the people of God. Led by the Priestly editors, in the effort to establish their identity as a religious rather than a national community, they went back beyond the conquest period to the time of Moses. "Thus the figure of Moses, who had always been revered . . . , became the prophet-mediator par excellence and exclusive . . . lawgiver."[5] The ancient "conquest fulfillment . . . no longer authenticated the identity of Judaism."[6]

The story of the Book of Joshua's displacement from the Torah demonstrates the importance of the role society played in the growth and development of the canon. It bears witness to the inseparability of the record of the Word of God from the history of the life of humanity. Just as the contents of the canon took shape around the faith of its writers, its limits were largely determined by the needs of its readers.

Interpretation

There are numerous ways of demonstrating the unbreakable connection between the personal history of the interpreter of God's Word and one's understanding of that Word. I propose to do it by a close analysis of the oft-used but rarely examined phrase, the "word of God." This loaded phrase consists of two principal components, *word* and *God*. The first stands for the familiar; the second, for the ultimate mystery. For while everybody knows what a word is, nobody knows exactly what God is. Consequently, when the two words are joined in a reference to ultimate reality, that does not strip the ultimate of all traces of mystery. Quite the contrary, it introduces the mystery of the ultimate, "God," into the familiar, "word."

Addition of the qualifier ". . . of God" to our description of the Bible as the "Word . . ." moves us to wonder if the Bible might not be quite impossible of interpretation. For who among us, since we all can only speak the language of human beings, can interpret the "Word of God"? How can we interpret God, the *transcendent reality*, without first ceasing to belong to that reality, temporal and spatial, which God transcends? In short, before we can interpret God, must we not cease to be human?

The Bible itself gives us the Christian basis for answering this question in the negative. In the life and ministry, the death and resurrection of Jesus Christ, God has given us the decisive and reliable clue to ultimate reality. If we would know how God feels about us or what God expects from us, we have but to look at the love and the life of Jesus. For this reason, the author of the Fourth Gospel, as have many other historians since, speaks of Jesus Christ as "the Word" that was with God from the very beginning.

When he speaks thus of God, this Evangelist raises the problem of distinguishing among the prophet's "Word of the Lord," the Bible as "the Word of God," and Christ as "the Word of God." What if one of the former represents the character or demand of God in a way that cannot be reconciled with the revelation of God in Jesus Christ? The Evangelist would not hesitate to identify the revelation of God in Christ as the standard for correction. Christ is not merely "the Word of God"; he is "the self-correcting Word of God." Christ is "the Word of God" by which all the other words of God, whether spoken by prophets or written in "the Book," must be judged. From here we are inevitably moved to ask, "Now that we have this definitive 'Word,' why should we bother any longer with these other words of God?"

The author of Hebrews hints at the answer to this question in his description of Jesus Christ as the same "yesterday, today, and forever." He did not, and would not, have said this of Jesus of Nazareth; he *was* but *is* no more. He belonged to the "flesh-and-blood" order which, Paul told the Galatians, cannot inherit the kingdom of God. But Jesus Christ, the revealer and agent of God, *was* and *is* and evermore *shall be.* When God in Christ confronts us in our place and time, God will reveal deity to us, as people came to know God in Jesus Christ, as a God of love.

But this "Word" of Christ, this "Word of God" for all time and every place, must not be restricted to any particular time or place. The God who spoke to Israel in the Exodus and to the new Israel in Jesus Christ is not a dead but a living God. God reigns *here* as God reigned there, *now* as God reigned then. Therefore, when we study the Scriptures, it is not merely or even primarily for the sake of finding out what God in Christ *was* like and *was* doing back then and there. Rather, it is for the sake of finding out what God *is* like and *is* doing in the here and now.

In other words, the proposition with which I launched

this point, "The Bible is the Word of God," is not a statement of fact. It is a confession of faith. Not a confession of faith in the Bible, but a confession of faith of God. It is our way of expressing the conviction that God now lives and loves, as in Jesus of Nazareth God once lived and loved, and that God still speaks, as through the prophets and apostles God once spoke, in the context of our own personal history.

The Inclusion of All Human Life and All the World in God's Word

No part of human life or the world can any more be omitted from the context of the Word of God than a part of human life or the world can excluded from the sovereignty of God. This assertion compels us to ask a couple of rather obvious questions. Do not other gods wield jurisdiction over parts of the world outside Palestine? And does not the Bible itself leave room for the segregation of segments of human life from the concern and dominion of Israel's God? An affirmative answer to either of these questions would open the way for biblical sanction of a very restricted view of the context of God's Word.

Recent biblical scholarship may not have clearly established the case for Moses as an explicit champion of theoretical monotheism, but it has done something far more important than that. It has left slight room for doubt that the people who defined the basic stance of Israel's prophetic faith were all alike, with no serious exception, contenders for the right of Yahweh (God) to exclusive claim on human obedience and service. To be sure, they did not always deny the existence of other gods. But they atoned for this oversight by so shrinking the boundaries of the power and influence of any other gods as to rob them of significant relevance for any part of our world.

The evidence for answering the question about the sovereignty of God over the whole of life is somewhat more ambiguous. Religion, in the view of certain biblical figures, had little to do with life outside the sanctuary. And God, as portrayed by these people, had equally little to do with anything but religion. Far from being alone, these persons seemed at times to enjoy the support of everybody but the dispossessed peasant and the lonely prophet. Yet the great prophets, to a person, scornfully repudiated this understanding of religion as a dreadful perversion. They produced a minority report in which they confronted their people with the demand for a radical choice. They did not call for a choice between religion and irreligion. They called, instead, for a choice between two quite different religions with two very different gods. One had its center and focus in the worship of a god as removed from human need as the sanctuary is removed from the marketplace. That was the popular religion of the pious masses. The other had its center and focus in the worship of a God as inseparable from human need as life from breathing. That was the unpopular religion of the great prophets.

Despite the assertion of Robert Martin-Achard that the Word of God "has nothing in common with any sort of . . . commercial enterprise,"[7] the biblical record of God's Word to human beings attests to the impossibility of ever disjoining it from God's Word about our economic life.

Since economic activity is an essential presupposition of human existence, it would be strange indeed, if God's Word had nothing to say about dispersion of the power that goes hand in hand with the acquisition, the use, and the disposition of property. Happily, there is no need for anxiety on this score. If here prophetic faith takes us by surprise, it will not be because of its indifference to this problem. Quite the contrary, it will be because of its obvious and potentially explosive relevance to our situation in relation to property.

It is interesting to note that Israelite legislation made quite specific provision for what we would call welfare cases.

80

Without pausing to ask why the poor got that way, it even took steps to reduce the ranks of the poor without resorting to the sanction of genocide. Every seventh year the fruit shall go to the poor (Exodus 23:10-11), Israel is told, so that there will be "no one in need among you" (see Deuteronomy 15:1-4).

As much as such charitable measures deserve our close study, they are not of primary importance. In fact, they pale into insignificance beside the attempt in Israel, through legislative action, to forestall the reduction of people to the level of poverty, or, in the case of escapees from that dread status, to prevent their return thereto. This was undoubtedly the motivation behind the requirement that compelled the person freeing a slave to provide him with enough property and goods for launching a successful start on an independent basis (Deuteronomy 15:12-18). Such prohibitions as those against the removal of a landmark (19:14) and the permanent sale of property outside the family without the right of redemption (Leviticus 25:25-28) must be understood in similar fashion. And the law of Levirate marriage (Deuteronomy 25:5-6) and the desire for male children were likewise intended as safeguards against the economic stratification of Israelite society.

The prophets did not take Israel's violation of these laws as evidence of their invalidity. They took it, instead, as proof of Israel's invalidation of the claim to be the irrevocably chosen people of God. And they turned it into a defense of their own anticipation of Israel's punishment at the hands, not of Egypt or Assyria or Babylon, but of God. The powerful rich had all too frequently gotten that way by treading roughshod over the broken bodies and crumpled dreams of the helpless poor. They had thereby disqualified themselves as the bearers of God's mission. They had converted the righteousness of God into their mortal enemy. Since their right to recognition as God's people carried with it a responsibility to respect the right of their neighbors to God's property, they left God

81

with no alternative. In the minds of Israel's great prophets, they left God with nothing to do but take his name away from them because they had taken God's property away from others.

The clear Word of the Lord demands of us, as Israel's prophets demanded of it, that either we abandon belief in God the Father and Owner, or else, distribute the treasures of earth so that they will bring joy to our Fatherly Owner and justice to God's beloved tenants. In short, it says that we cannot truly affirm the fatherhood of God without advancing the familyhood of humanity.

Martin-Achard claims the same irrelevance of God's Word for political activity as he claimed for commercial activity. It has "nothing in common with it,"[8] he declares. If I shared this conviction, I would have to question the relevance of the Word of God for the workaday world of modern humanity. Despite the repeated and tragic failures of modern politics, I would still contend that what we need today is not less but better politics. And so, too, would the so-called theologians of the secular. Alert to the church's supreme opportunity and her tragic unpreparedness to grasp it, they do a lot of talking these days about the sacralization of politics. They acknowledge the necessity of effecting a reconciliation between God and government, piety and power, justification and justice. But how, given our history in the United States of the separation of church and state, not to mention the separation of tithes and taxes, and the New Testament's apparent aversion to the exercise of political power, do we bring this to pass? To what source do we turn in search of a precedent in attacking this problem?

That source is as near as the textbook of the prophetic faith of Israel. From there I could document the inseparable connection between religion and politics at great length, but I shall confine myself to a single illustration of its sanction of the use of political power. Consider the prophet Jeremiah's contrasting opinion of two Judahite kings. As if a king could do no right, he flayed Jehoiakim in wholly raucous tones and terms, contemptuously promising him the burial of an ass. On the other hand, as if a king could only do right, he praised Josiah in wholly warm and approving tones and terms. Jeremiah did not praise Josiah because of the latter's disdain for the use of power. For seldom, if ever, had Judah known a king who threw his weight around in a wider circle or with more enthusiasm. Jeremiah praised Josiah, not for his refusal of power, but for his use of power, for his enlistment of power on the side of "the poor and needy" (Jeremiah 22:16) and in pursuit of "justice and righteousness" (22:15).

Despite the fact that kings like Josiah played a decisive role in causing the messianic hope to take shape around the "son of David" title, we Christians, almost from the very beginning, have virtually ignored the political dimension of this expectation. Even though our ancestors in the faith were quick to claim the title of messiah for Jesus of Nazareth, they were equally quick to deny him a role that had any political significance, either for his day or ours. Surely one does not have to be a psychic to foresee the outcome of our failure to correct this oversight. For if it is allowed to go uncorrected, the religion with which we confront humanity shall continue to be something less than fully potent, a great deal less than sufficiently muscular, and tragically less than equal to the demands of God or the needs of humanity in the midst of an organizational and technological revolution. By the same token, if we manage to close the gap between the kingdom of this world and the reign of God, it will be in spite of our religion, not on account of it.

This is not an easy time for us, prophet-like, to proclaim the Word of God in terms of the use of power. It may turn out to be just as dangerous as it was for the prophets of Israel to try to bring politics under the umbrella of God's Word. But if we are going to stake out God's claim in "the secular city," this is a risk we shall have to take.

Without a doubt, we could document the case for the exclusion of large chunks of human life from the sovereignty of God, but we had better pause for a second look at the sources from which we would have to do it. For unless we are prepared to reject out of hand both the foundations of faith laid by Israel's great prophets and the superstructure raised thereon by Jesus and his disciples, we have no alternative but to affirm the lordship of God over both the whole world and the whole of our life in the world. By the same token, given God's rule as the ground and goal of revelation, whether to the prophets of ancient Israel or the modern United States, the context of God's Word must be drawn in an equally wide circle. In short, if that Word be anything less than a demand for the transformation of both the whole world and the whole of our life in the world into a sacrament of the divine presence and purpose, we must doubt both its source and its spokespersons.

The Surprising Character of God's Word

Granted a dynamic understanding of history, we dare not write the future of the Word of God on the basis of the past of the Word of God. To do so would be tantamount not only to denying the dynamic character of the Word of God itself; in effect, it would also be tantamount to denying God the power to say or do anything that God has not already said or done. It would be to enhance the written Word of God at the expense of the living Word of God.

The danger of this approach becomes clear in the Old Testament studies that not only organize the materials of the Hebrew Bible around the central events in ancient Israelite history but also proceed, in light of these same events, to deduce their theological significance for us and the ancient Israelites.[9] Ironically, most of the Old Testament scholars adopting this approach would maintain not only that they take history seriously but that they interpret it dynamically. They identify the encounter between the constant—the divine sovereignty, and the variable—the human response, as the matrix out of which comes the new and the unpredictable—that is, the open future.[10] Nevertheless, in some instances where this approach prevails, the selection of events belies the contingent view of history implied in the foregoing concept of the future. Where this happens, when modern interpreters write thus of an open future,[11] they are talking about our future, not that of the ancient Israelite.

Although the number and choice of events may vary from writer to writer, those selected by B. Davie Napier illustrate this method and its misleading implications. Besides the Exodus from Egypt, the establishment of the Davidic monarchy, and the exile of Samaria and Judah, Napier includes anticipation of the fulfillment of the covenant.[12] Each of these events, because of its decisive place in the history of Israel, can doubtless contribute greatly to our understanding of the meaning of Israelite history. Yet the first three of these events as concrete happenings in space and time have a place in the reconstruction of Israelite history before they happened, only to the extent that they were anticipated by Israelites prior to their occurrence. Despite "the characteristic ways in which things happen and interaction takes place, . . . because men are free and creative, no certain predictions can be based on them."[13] To contend otherwise would be to forgo a dynamic view of history. Unless we are willing to deny the freedom to human beings in which every dynamic view of history roots, every past event must be viewed as a contingent development. Certainly such an event has no place whatever in any study purporting to be at all historical. At that time it marked only one of numerous possibilities, any one of which might have robbed it of its place in history. In other words, the rise of Christianity no more belongs to the reconstruction of the Jewish exile in Babylon, or the conquest of David to the story of the escape of Israel from Egypt than the war between the United States and Russia for control of Mars belongs to the record of

World War III. If we would take human freedom and history seriously, we must refuse to treat any event that has yet to take place as if it had already taken place.

Without question, if historians were to take human freedom and human history with utmost seriousness, the story of the past, and most especially the story of our religious past, would become a far less smooth and a far more suspenseful story. By the same token, if we Christians were to take the historical character of Christianity with utmost seriousness, we would stop trying to confine *life in faith* to the forms in which our ancestors have transmitted the faith to us. Certainly Christian history offers strong support for reversing this process. Instead of the forms of faith, including those we meet in the Bible, creating the life of faith, it was the other way around. The life of faith inspired and gave shape to the forms of faith.

Any serious appropriation of this insight, far from reducing the importance of the search for the historical context of the Bible, would make that search all the more important. For granted the fact that words have a history and often undergo changes in meaning in the course of history, we need to put not less but more emphasis on the search for the historical context of biblical terms and titles. And furthermore, granted that what we get in the New Testament is the presentation of the transcendent in terms of the historical, we are challenged to explore the historical context of the background and use of all such terms and titles. This challenge holds not only for such concepts as those of virgin birth, transfiguration and resurrection. It also holds for every title and record purporting to describe the action of God in nature or history.

To suppose, therefore, that the future of genuine faith hinges on the literal transmission of any biblical term, be it "messiah" (from the Hebrew) or "Christ" (from the Greek) or the language of the inherited creeds, would be to reduce biblical-Christian faith to a mystery religion in which the possession of secret knowledge holds the key to salvation. Or to suppose that we can say something of Christ that cannot be

86

said, with equal accuracy, of the God of creation, marks an expression, not of full-orbed Trinitarianism, but of a unitarianism of the second person of the Trinity. And an equally negative judgment had to be passed on the view that would deny the possibility of salvation for persons who hesitate to employ our favorite titles for God, even though they ascribe to deity the love revealed in Jesus Christ and live lives of Christlike obedience and service. Such exclusivism suggests that Jesus Christ of Nazareth would take offense if we Christians were to assemble fellow believers under the name of the God of Abraham, Isaac and Jacob or, for that matter, the God of creation. However, as Gregory Dix reminds us:

> When Christians took to calling Jesus Lord instead of Messiah, the Liberals wrongly supposed that they were "heightening the Christology." The point is that Jewish messianism does not yield a Christology of status in metaphysical terms it yields a Christology of function in terms of history. But the function of the Messiah is undoubtedly a divine function, . . . namely (the) inauguration of God's Kingdom. The messiah's action in history is God's own action.[14]

The Old Testament God of our creation is identical with the New Testament God of our redemption. Therefore, if and when we identify believers in such a manner as to exclude from the people of God the Redeemer those who belong to the people of God the Creator, we challenge the Christology of the Gospels and the Christian doctrine of the Trinity in one and the same breath. All persons share a common humanity, irrespective of whether they presently do, or ever shall, share in common "one faith" or "one baptism" (Ephesians 4:5). And they may share a common life in faith without being able to subscribe to a common formulation of the faith.

The last book penned by my teacher and one-time colleague, Nels Ferré, bore the title of The Universal Word.[15] He came to the conclusion that the Word that became flesh in

Jesus of Nazareth was one with the Word that was "in the beginning" (John 1:1) via an exercise in philosophical deduction. I have moved in exactly the opposite direction. Via an exercise in historical induction, I have moved from the unique Word of God revealed in the Bible to a plea for acknowledgment of its universal implications. Therefore, despite our agreement as to the dynamic and surprising character of the Word of God, I would not trace this apparent similarity in our conclusions to the influence of his teaching. I would credit it, instead, to my studied effort to take history with utmost seriousness in my analysis of the Word of God. Indeed, I do not see how any fair-minded interpreter, aware of the variety of ways in which the Word of God manifests itself in the Bible, could analyze that word in historical context and not conclude, with Karl Rahner that "even with regard to his salvation, . . . even here man must rely on concrete history with its successive phases."[16]

Rahner stops short of saying that the content of the Word of God, save only for purposes of analysis, cannot and should not be separated from either its context or its communication. But then he did not have my topic as the immediate stimulus for writing the essay from which I have just quoted. Had he been thus focused, I have no doubt that he, too, would have contended for the unity of the content, the communication, and the context of the Word of God. Indeed, the notion that we can separate the content and communication of the Word from its context belies the biblical witness to revelation as a very specific and concrete encounter between Creator and creatures in the struggle and uncertainty of human history as we know it.

Conclusion

Declaring that, biblically speaking, our life and history have no meaning apart from God's Word is a truism. But it is no less a truism to say that the Bible knows no other Word of God than that which was spoken and heard in the life and history of human beings. Therefore if we would take the Bible seriously, we must listen for and respond to God's Word as the writers of the Bible did. Or to put it differently, we must worship the Lord over history by heeding the Lord in history—that is, by listening for and acting upon God's Word about life as God speaks it to us in the midst of our living. The Word of God is not our guide to where the action *was*. It is our guide to where the action *is*.

The specific communication between God and humanity, the prior concern for the world over concern for the church, the inseparability of the good life from the good things of life, the impossibility of a divorce of politics from economics—each and all of these insights are characteristic of vital religion in this generation. I am not prepared to document the significance of this fact by defining how the Bible should be read in U.S. culture.

Of this one thing, however, I am sure: If we seek to enter into dialogue with the God of the prophets and apostles without due regard for these insights, we will betray more than our mission. We will betray the children of our God. We will betray the God of the prophets and apostles, the Father of our Lord Jesus Christ.

Questions for Discussion

1. How does God's revelation come to us through the human beings who spoke and wrote the material that has become the Bible? How is God's communication to us affected by these human "instruments"?

2. How is our understanding of the Bible enhanced by some knowledge of the process by which the scriptural canon(s) was (were) shaped? Does John Wesley's under-

standing of "double inspiration" (in the Witherington chapter) offer us help here?

3. Tilson insists that the authentic religion of the biblical/Christian tradition cannot be separated from economic, commercial, and political concerns. What evidence can you cite for or against this position? If Tilson is right, how should this influence our personal and corporate practices as Christians?

4. What aspects of Tilson's chapter did you find (a) most helpful, (b) most difficult, (c) most surprising?

Chapter 4

Characteristics of United Methodist Study and Interpretation of the Bible

Gayle Carlton FELTON

Is THERE A distinctively United Methodist way of reading, studying, and interpreting the Bible? In many senses the answer to this question must be acknowledged to be "no." United Methodists claim not only no monopoly on biblical knowledge but also not even any superiority in biblical understanding. What we do claim is a vital interest in the Holy Scripture and deep respect for its teachings in matters of faith and morals.

Clues as to what may be distinctive about how United Methodists approach the Bible may be gleaned from an examination of some distinguishing characteristics of our denomination's theology and practice. The heritage of United Methodism was received from its founder John Wesley and passed on through the churches that make up the denomination today. It is a heritage that can perhaps most accurately be described as *mediating*—one in which diverse aspects of the Christian tradition are held together. At best, these various elements create a rich, balanced synthesis; at worst, they constitute fuel for church family feuding. Let us consider three aspects of this mediating heritage.

First, from John Wesley, the Anglican priest, we inherit

appreciation for "high church" liturgy, ritual, and sacrament. From Wesley, the outdoor-preaching evangelist, we inherit emphasis upon conversion, repentance, and personal faith in Christ.

Second, we are the heirs of a theology based firmly upon the reality of divine grace, freely available to all persons. This gift of grace, however, must be accepted by the human response of faith if it is to be effectual in our lives. Third, we receive from our forebears a legacy of personal piety and holiness, kept alive and growing through spiritual disciplines. This is coupled with stress upon the necessity of good works, caring for the needy, and peace and justice action toward holiness for the whole of society. Much of the dissension, confusion, and dilemma of contemporary United Methodism is the outcome of attempting to rip apart these vital elements of our tradition and elevate one or another of them at the expense of the rest. The mutilated identity, murky message, and muddled mission that result are devoid of power to save souls and redeem the world for Christ.

How is this mediating and endangered heritage of United Methodism relevant to our subject here—how we study and interpret the Bible? We need to be reminded that the Bible belongs to the church. It is the product of the work of God's people over the centuries—experiencing, recording, interpreting, teaching, applying, and transmitting the divine revelation. The Bible tells us who God is and who we are in relation to God, to others, and to the natural environment. Biblical truth is proclaimed in the church's corporate worship—in liturgy, ritual, music, and sacraments—and in the more obvious acts of Scripture reading and preaching. The Old and New Testaments relate the story of God's continuing action to reach out with saving grace to human beings who have separated themselves from God by their acts of disobedience. While God pursues and woos, humankind must respond with acceptance and faith to God's gracious offer of salvation. As Wesley affirmed, the Bible is one of the means of grace given to us as vehicles or channels through which the active love of God comes into our lives. When we allow grace to claim our lives and to begin to transform us, we find that God will make us increasingly into the image of Christ. This holiness of life will be expressed in personal piety nourished by intentional spiritual disciplines and expressed in lives of service to others.

The Challenge of Interpreting the Bible

United Methodists today are showing great interest in learning more about and from the Bible. Many are disturbed, even embarrassed, by their lack of knowledge and are hungry to study and learn. The biblical and theological illiteracy characteristic of so much of our culture, even of our churchgoing people, both frustrates and challenges the church. Respect for the Bible is pervasive and deep; understanding of it is too often both narrow and shallow. I grew up in the Bible Belt of the South where I was taught to revere the Bible as a book. Always it was to be on top of any stack of books; never was it to be placed on the floor. I remember how uncomfortable I was in an introductory college class when the instructor told us to underline and make written notes on the pages of our Bibles. I observed this same discomfort in my students when I taught such introductory Bible classes almost three decades later. Unfortunately such veneration for the Bible as an object does not easily translate into critical study and profound insight into its contents. Indeed, such attitudes may actually inhibit fruitful scriptural study and encourage instead a kind of idolatry that reduces Christians to Bible-worshipers rather than followers of Christ.

The last decades of the twentieth century witnessed an unhappy resurgence of misunderstanding and misuse of the Bible, especially on the part of some who would call themselves conservatives, but who are usually deemed by those with whom they disagree as fundamentalists. Perhaps the clearest examples of this development are to be seen in the actions of the Southern Baptist Convention. In 1984, the SBC recommended that its constituent congregations stop the practice of ordaining women to ministry. This pronouncement was justified by citing 1 Timothy 2:12-15. In 1998, the SBC, grounding its action in Ephesians 5:22-24, asserted that wives are to be graciously submissive to their husbands. These instances are of interest to United Methodists because they are so blatant and have received so much publicity. Conservative opinions within our denomination tend to be expressed more subtly and to focus more on economic, political, and social issues, rather than on domestic ones. The most salient example is the ongoing controversy over homosexuality.

On the grassroots, person-in-the-pew, and sometimes person-in-the-pulpit level, this conservative/fundamentalist view of the Bible is colloquially expressed as, "The Bible says it; I believe it; that settles it!" The obvious problem, of course, is that this approach is not only naively simplistic, but worse, it is demonstrably unworkable. Put more bluntly, such a view is not only wrong, but also impossible to sustain! A much more sophisticated statement of the inerrancy view of the Bible was developed by Presbyterian scholars at Princeton Theological School in the late nineteenth century: "when all the facts are known, the Scriptures in their original autographs and properly interpreted, will be shown to be wholly true in everything that they affirm, whether that has to do with doctrine or morality or with the social, physical or life sciences."[1] The Bible is here being asserted as accurate and authoritative not only in the sphere of religious matters, but also in fields such as history, geology, and biology. Notice that the statement is bristling with qualifiers and limitations. "All the facts" are very unlikely to ever be known, at least in this life; no original autographs (copies) of any biblical book are known to be in existence; the issue of proper interpretation is perhaps the pivotal question of the entire controversy. In reality, the statement is so hypothetical as to be meaningless.

Why are simplistic beliefs about the clear assertions and absolute authority of the Bible so popular and widespread? There are at least two reasons. One is the attraction of a pious position that appears to offer the security of ready answers to life's troubling questions. It is very comforting to many people to be able to believe that they have easy access to a reliable source that contains the unchanging truth about God's way and will. People in the United States often insist that they want the freedom to think and decide for themselves, but in reality, in matters of faith many prefer the perceived safety of being told what to believe and do. Second, because the church has done such a poor job of teaching, many Christians who are uncomfortable with these simplistic views are ill-equipped to formulate other creditable, defensible positions. For example, I have seen this dilemma in United Methodist congregations who have received an ordained woman as their pastor. Even when the members of the congregation are themselves supportive of their clergy woman's ministry, they find themselves unable to counter the proof-texting criticism from their conservative relatives and friends. Sensing that there are better ways to understand the Scripture, but ignorant of what they are, United Methodists may find themselves without answers to questions such as, "Can't you people read the Bible? Don't you know that God says women shouldn't be preachers?" We could, of course, multiply examples and issues.

The responsibility for teaching United Methodist people how to read, study, and interpret the Bible ultimately falls on the ordained deacons and elders. It is they who have the duty of equipping the laity for their own ministries of witnessing, teaching, and serving. Laypeople are, in general, eager to learn and open to fresh ideas presented appropriately. I have on numerous occasions in my own ministry of teaching laity, been asked the haunting question, "Why didn't anybody ever tell us this before?" Writing in a popular magazine for United Methodist clergy, Phil Wogaman, pastor of Foundry United Methodist Church in Washington, DC, relates similar experiences. His article is entitled "It's Time for You to Tell the Truth."[2] Wogaman asserts that often pastors are reluctant to share their own knowledge of the Bible with their congregations for fear of setting off controversy: "The result is that generation after generation of Christians are deprived of the opportunity to understand and express their faith with intellectual maturity." There is little value in the prodigious amounts of time, energy, efforts, and money spent for and by theological schools to train students in biblical knowledge and interpretation if those students cannot or will not go into churches as pastors who communicate to their people what they have learned. Too often our pastors are both unwilling to risk dissension and incapable of effective teaching of the Word. Wogaman asks:

> Are we in the UMC really able to speak to the vast numbers of people who are earnestly seeking truth and values on which they can base their lives? When such people look to the church, what do they see? Surely they cannot expect to find ready-made answers to every question here, for the church will struggle with its own understanding of truth until the end of time. But will the church be a place for such people to address their own questions honestly because the church is honest about its own sources and traditions as well as honest in its interpretation of the age in which it lives? How much will the best of our young people have to unlearn when they encounter the mainstream of knowledge away from the bosom of the church?[3]

The salient problem with inerrancy and infallibility approaches to understanding the Bible is that they simply will not work! There is no real option of "just believing what the Bible says," because, in truth, the Bible says a variety of things on the same issues. This can be illustrated by an array of examples. First, there are numerous historical problems. In Matthew 27:5, Judas is said to have hanged himself; in Acts 1:18, the manner of his death is described quite differently—and much more gorily. Perusal of the genealogies of Jesus as they appear in Matthew 1 and in Luke 3 reveals significant contrast, even contradiction. Second, the inerrantist approach cannot accommodate factual problems in the scriptural text, such as the conflicting accounts in the Four Gospels concerning the beings who were seen at Jesus' tomb—Matthew (28:2) says one angel; Mark (16:5), a young man; Luke (24:4), two men; and John (20:12), two angels. Perhaps more problematic for the casual reader, is some of the "theology" of biblical writers—Ecclesiastes 2:24a, "There is nothing better for mortals than to eat and drink, and find enjoyment in their toil"; and 3:19-20, "For the fate of humans and the fate of animals is the same; as one dies, so dies the other. They all have the same breath, and humans have no advantage over the animals; for all is vanity. All go to one place; all are from the dust, and all turn to dust again."

Most distressing are passages of Scripture that appear to speak with approval of actions that are clearly immoral—Psalm 137:9, "Happy shall they be who take your little ones and dash them against the rock!"; Genesis 19:8 in which Lot offers his two virgin daughters to the rapacious mob; Judges 19 which tells the story of the Levite who threw his concubine to a similar mob who "wantonly raped her, and abused her all through the night . . ."; the rape law of ancient Israel, in Deuteronomy 22:28-29, by which a virgin woman who has been raped is bound in the lifelong servitude of marriage to her rapist, while her father collects fifty shekels of silver! To point out that many of these passages are from the Old Testament does nothing to protect the inerrantist, especially since many of the passages cited in present-day debates, over abortion and homosexuality for examples, are from the Old Testament as well.

It should never be our purpose simply to tear down the old opinions and understandings that people have of the Bible. Indeed, it is truly wrong to destroy anything upon which an individual's faith rests, unless and until we are prepared to guide them to understandings that are better. Our purpose must be to enrich people's study and interpretation of the Bible and, in so doing, encourage deeper commitment to the Christian faith and lives of more responsible Christian discipleship. How can we enable persons to allow the Bible to function authoritatively in their personal and public lives without viewing it rigidly as inerrant factual truth? How can we help Christians to distinguish between the inspiration of the Holy Spirit and printer's ink on onionskin paper?

The Word of God in Human Packaging

Repeatedly in the chapters of this book, the phrase "the Word of God" recurs. The issue of how United Methodist Christians can most faithfully study and understand the Bible turns on the meanings of this phrase. For us as human beings and for God, *word* connotes a form of expression, a medium of communication. It is by our words that we share our ideas with others, that we relate information about who we are, that we learn about and from others. Words have a dual power for us—they not only express our thoughts, but also shape our thinking. (This is why language that is inclusive in terms of gender, ethnicity, and other human differences is so important.) The Word of God in the Bible is both a record of God's revelation of the divine self to human beings, and a vehicle through which that revelation continues. Better than asserting that the Bible *is* God's Word, is to understand that the Bible *contains* God's Word. Indeed, the Bible can be characterized as containing God's Word in human packaging. The divine Word is eternal truth, universal and unchanging, relevant to the life of God's creatures in all its manifold diversity. The human packaging in which the divine Word is encased is, by contrast, temporal, culturally conditioned, limited by the weaknesses of its human agents.

Studying and interpreting the Bible can be viewed as the process of unwrapping the human packaging in order to discover the Word of God that it contains.

It is tempting, although surely futile, to speculate about why God chose this method for self-revelation. It seems that it would have been so much simpler for us if God had actually dictated the divine message to robotic human recorders! Instead however, the reality with which we have to contend is that God used human beings writing in their own languages within their own circumstances and expressing themselves in their particular historical and cultural settings. The result is that "we have this treasure in clay jars" (2 Corinthians 4:7). Perhaps it is that God, knowing very well the capacities of the human creatures God makes, designs that we utilize our intellectual and our spiritual gifts to apprehend the Word that God makes available to us.

I have a poster depicting the crucified Christ with the caption "Jesus came to take away your sins, not your mind!" This perspective on Scripture leaves plenty of room for divine inspiration. One of the meanings of the word *inspire* is "to breathe into." The divine Word was breathed into human agents when it was experienced and recorded; it was transmitted through the centuries by human processes that were guided and guarded by the Holy Spirit; it is read, studied, and interpreted today as in the past through the wisdom and insight that come from the Holy Spirit. We can most effectively unveil the Word of God to our understanding as we learn as much as we can about the human packaging in which it comes to us.

One component of that packaging is the genre or literary type of biblical books and passages. The Bible comes to us not as systematic theology, but as great literature. It may be best characterized as an anthology containing a variety of types of literature. Helpfully, the biblical books are arranged in an order that reflects their predominant genre. One can divide the Bible's table of contents to show these major groupings. The first five books of the Old Testament—the Torah or Pentateuch—are classified as books of law, although they also contain much history. The twelve books from Joshua through Esther are historical; they are followed by five books of poetry, ending with Song of Solomon. The remainder of the Old Testament is made up of books of prophecy (with the exception of Daniel, which is apocalyptic); these books are, in general, arranged in order of their length rather than their content.

The New Testament begins with the Four Gospels (the Synoptics and John); followed by Acts, which is history; and the twenty-one epistles, also arranged mainly according to length. Revelation is apocalyptic literature, which deals with the end times of history. Obviously not all of these can be studied and understood in the same way. Knowing the genre of what is being read enables the reader to know how to approach interpreting it. This means that the Bible does not, and is not supposed to, function like a reference book of some sort where one might go to find a specific subject or to locate a discussion on a particular theological point. Neither is the Bible to be used like a recipe book to tell us how to make something happen or like a telephone directory where we seek specific bits of information. Illustrations of the point are endless, but some of my favorites include Job 38, which surely ranks, even in translation, as some of the finest poetry ever penned. The dramatic collection of legends about Samson in the Book of Judges most likely developed as the people of Israel were struggling, often with little success, against the oppression of the Philistines. The beautiful myths in the early chapters of Genesis are foundational to our understanding of the remainder of the Bible. While not intended to be historical or scientific, they convey universal truth that is deeper than facts.

Another and perhaps more obvious aspect of the human packaging in which the biblical Word of God is contained is the symbolic, figurative language with which it is replete. People will sometimes say that they "take the Bible literally," but in truth it is extremely doubtful that anyone really does so. When Isaiah 55:12 says that "the mountains and the hills before you shall burst into song, and all the trees of the field shall clap their hands," does any reader take this literally? Examples of the use of such language can be found in most biblical books; metaphor, simile, analogy, and hyperbole are types of figures of speech that the biblical writers used extensively, as do creative authors in any time and culture. The parables of Jesus are good illustrations; in a few cases, notably the parable of the sower, the story is very close to an allegory (Matthew 13:3-8 and parallels). Much pointless effort could be spared if readers would recognize, for example, that when Jesus spoke of a camel going through the eye of a needle (Luke 18:25 and parallels) he was engaging in typical Middle Eastern hyperbole, not referring to some unusual geological formation in the area. Interestingly, the author of the Gospel of John uses the shortsighted literalness of Jesus' hearers as a literary device unifying the whole book. Repeatedly Jesus speaks to his disciples and to the crowds in figures of speech, and repeatedly they misunderstand his meaning because they try to take him literally. This motif sets up opportunities for Jesus to explain himself more fully and provides the occasions for some of his most profound teachings. Excellent specimens are found in John 4:14; 6:52-54; 15:1ff.; and, indeed, throughout this Gospel.

Still another expression of the human packaging of Scripture can be seen when one contrasts the Word of God delivered in a specific historical situation to that enunciated in another time and circumstance. A striking example of this is found by comparing Isaiah 2:4 with Joel 3:9-10. The familiar Isaiah text envisions the beating of "swords into plowshares and spears into pruning hooks." The lesser-known Joel text picks up on this prophetic word of the great Isaiah and turns it on its head. Joel is recognizing the contrast between the historical situation of his own day and that of Isaiah's time. Accordingly he exhorts the people to, "Beat your plowshares into swords, and your pruning hooks into spears." Without some knowledge of the historical setting of these prophecies, the contradiction between them is inexplicable. Certainly these two passages alone offer sufficient evidence of the insufficiency of the old "the Bible says it; I believe it" viewpoint. Two other contrasting passages should be cited, especially for their relevance to our contemporary political debate about capital punishment. Many Christians quote Exodus 21:23-25 to argue that God's justice demands "life for life, eye for eye" Amazingly, these Christians ignore Matthew 5:38-41 in which Jesus himself nullifies the Exodus passage and advocates nonresistance and nonretaliation. It may well be that neither of these passages contains the answer to our capital punishment dilemma, but it should surely be clear that we cannot in good conscience value the Old Testament directive above the words of Christ himself.

Because the biblical authors were real human beings, their writings reflect their personal opinions and experiences as part of the packaging we are attempting to unwrap. In 2 Samuel 24:1 it is said that "the LORD" motivated David to take a census of the people of Israel. The author of 1 Chronicles 21:1, writing from the perspective of some five hundred years later, knew that the census was used as a tool for heavy taxation and forced labor. This author's view of the census is in keen opposition to that of the earlier historian. The Chronicler attributed the motivation for the census to "Satan," rather than to God.

Probably the most influential factor in shaping the human packaging of the divine Word was the cultural conditions and social practices of the times out of which the various books of the biblical canon developed. There are vast differences between the worlds of the biblical writers and the world in which contemporary United Methodists live as we enter the twenty-first century. While this certainly does not mean that the Bible is without relevance to us today, it does mean that we must be aware of pervasive and profound disparities that must be reckoned with as we study, interpret, and apply Scripture today. In actuality, all readers of the Bible make distinctions between those portions that they deem to be so culturally conditioned as to be without importance for present-day Christians and those portions that they believe to continue to be authoritative.

Very few Christians feel themselves bound to make their food choices according to the dietary dictates in the eleventh chapter of Leviticus. Even fewer refuse to wear clothing made of combinations of fibers, as decreed in Deuteronomy 22:11. Although the world of the New Testament is much closer to us in terms of centuries than that of the Old, it too reflects the presuppositions and values of cultures radically different from our own. The teaching about proper head coverings in 1 Corinthians 11:4-15 expresses the thought of a society so unlike our own that we cannot comprehend what it is that Paul was trying to convey. The admonitions to slaves in Ephesians 6:5-8 were an exceedingly popular text for white preachers in the antebellum South, but they strike today's Christians as morally repugnant. In short, the cultural and social settings in which the writers of the Bible lived were characterized by conditions that we find difficult to comprehend and surely would not wish to replicate.

The chief challenge of biblical study and interpretation, then, is to learn to differentiate between that which is human, time-bound, culturally restricted, and that which is divine, eternal, and universal. In order to be able to do this responsibly, we must learn all that we can about every aspect of the biblical setting. We need to ask and be able to

103

answer the question, "What did this passage mean to the community to whom it was originally addressed?" Only then can we proceed to ask and hope to apprehend, "What does this passage mean to us today?" Fortunately, it is not required that we be scholars of the Scripture in the academic sense. It *is* essential that we be students of the Word in the spiritual sense. As students, we need to engage the scriptural text in dialogue, asking questions, probing possibilities, forming and discarding hypotheses, pressing toward deeper insight. God's Word is honored by our relentless efforts toward understanding and application. God is revered, not threatened, when we concentrate our finest abilities on seeking to know and to become involved in the divine will and purpose. We are to apply ourselves to the Word with diligence, using our best capacities and resources to search for riches in its depths. If we do, we have the promise of the presence and assistance of the Holy Spirit—the same Spirit who inspired the authors will guide the readers.

The Challenge of Understanding the Interpreter

Just as the Bible was not written in a supernaturally imposed vacuum, so it cannot be read in isolation from human factors of influence. As we as readers and interpreters seek to comprehend the Bible and apply it to our individual and corporate lives, we must be knowledgeable also about ourselves. No one can read Scripture from a totally objective perspective. All of us are somebody in particular; we are not simply neutral readers. Just as we need to be aware of the personal opinions and experiences, the historical situations, and the cultural conditions of those who wrote the Word, we must be aware of these same factors in all who read it. The Bible comes to us not only wrapped in the human packaging of its authors and their worlds but also subject to unwrapping by other persons who are fully as human and, most likely, less open to divine inspiration.

A very valuable section in Volume 1 of *The New Interpreter's Bible* begins with an article entitled "Reading the Bible From Particular Social Locations: An Introduction." James Earl Massey opens with these statements: "Interpretation of the Bible depends largely on the social perspectives of the interpreter. This statement should not surprise, because whether one is dealing with Holy Writ or any other written materials, there is usually some influence on our thinking from the sociocultural setting that has affected our lives."[4] I would differ from Massey only in believing that there is *always* some sociocultural influence upon our interpretation. This is not to argue that the power of the Holy Spirit cannot and does not sometimes enable us to transcend these influences. It is to contend that the same God who has chosen to encase the divine Word in the trappings of human authors, chooses also to so encase its interpretation. God apparently has great confidence in God's creatures!

The United Methodist tradition has historically sought to remain grounded in the realities of historical situation and cultural context. We read the Scripture as Protestants in the United States in and of our own time. We read it as women or men; as persons of diverse races and ethnicities, sexual orientations, socioeconomic class, educational backgrounds, age categories, and a myriad of more subtle distinctions. These diverse, and sometimes divergent, strands are to be interwoven into a rich fabric of meaning. Perhaps this is part of what it means to interpret the Bible in the community of faith. No one of us, or single grouping of us, has the capacity to comprehend God's Word alone. The divine voice speaks to us out of the dialogue in which we engage with those who differ from us.

The danger that continually besets us is that of failing to recognize that our perspective is *a* perspective, not *the* perspective. I have often asked my students to compare two hypothetical history textbooks on the subject of the war that occurred in the United States between 1861 and 1865—one published in Boston and one in Atlanta, both in 1870. Quickly the contrast in context becomes clear. Not only are the battles called by different names, but the war that the Boston book called "The Civil War" is likely in the Atlanta book to be designated "The War Between the States" or even "The War of Northern Aggression"! These distinctions are more than simply matters of nomenclature—they express contrasting understandings of what the war itself was all about. And, what comparison would we be able to make between the chapters in two such books entitled "Causes of the Conflict"? The point is obvious when one looks at an example like this. The determinative influence of context is not always so apparent in matters of biblical interpretation, but it is just as real. This must not be understood as an argument that there is no objective reality or absolute truth. I believe that there is—both about the Civil War and about the Scripture. What I do not believe is that any one individual or group has exclusive possession of such truth and that it is not only intellectual but also spiritual arrogance to so claim. We must be willing to listen to and learn from one another, to share our experience and insight, to respect one another's context, and to be cognizant of our own. There is no "Christian" interpretation of the Bible on one hand, with feminist, gay, black, liberationist, and other interpretations on the other. Similarly, there is no "Christian" theology, as opposed to specific theologies—feminist, gay, black, and so forth. What is often termed "Christian" represents the experience and perspective of specific groups who have been, and largely continue to be, dominant in the culture—white (European origin), male, middle and upper class, educated. Authentically Christian biblical understanding requires blending the voices of all God's diverse people.

Themes in the Biblical Story

Much of the lack of comprehension and appreciation for the Scripture may stem from the piecemeal approach of too many readers. Typically, individual Christians have their own favorite passages that they know well and use often. What is frequently missing is a coherent view of the whole Bible—a sense of the sweep of the narrative from Genesis through Revelation. For this reason, many Christians are unclear about the significance of the Old Testament and its relationship to the New; they find it difficult and confusing; they avoid reading (and in the case of pastors, preaching) most parts of it.

United Methodists are heirs of a Protestant tradition that recognizes that, despite its enormous diversity, the Bible ultimately tells one story. That story is about God—the only true God—and God's dealings with humankind throughout the centuries since creation and until the final consummation of history. Through this story we learn who God is and who we are, God's purpose for humanity and action to achieve that purpose, and our identity and mission as people of God.

A helpful way of approaching the Scripture is to view it as the story of three orders of existence. First is the created order that is described in Genesis 1 and 2. Here we learn that the universe is the result of God's intentional act of creation. All that God created is good. The created order is characterized by harmony, peace, intimacy, abundance, and equality. Human life is lived as the Creator intended, by creatures made in the image of God. The second order of existence commences in the third chapter of Genesis with the intrusion of sin into God's good creation. Sin results from human misuse of the gift of free will. God's human creatures refuse to accept God's will and way. They invent new values; they rebel and disobey; they indulge their own selfish interests.

As a result of this fall into sin, the qualities of the created order are lost, human life is radically altered, and the image of God is defaced. Sinful human beings experience a three-fold estrangement. They are alienated from one another (Genesis 3:12, 16); from the natural environment (3:14-15, 17-19, 23); and most sadly, from their Creator (3:8, 23-24). All of human history has been lived in this fallen order of existence. What is, is not what God intends. The fallen order is characterized by strife, violence, hatred, scarcity, and hierarchy. But God does not give up on creation! The rest of the entire Bible is the account of God's relentless pursuit, of God's ongoing effort to reconcile and restore, of God's gracious initiative, of God's unyielding determination to rescue and redeem. By divine action, this fallen order in which we live is being undermined by the third order of existence, which is better called the redeeming order than the redeemed. God is at work and calling human creatures to join in the task. God ultimately will reestablish the wholeness and goodness of the created order. The divine purpose will be actualized. In the Bible we are given glimpses of what this redeemed order will look like. In Isaiah 9:1-7 and 11:1-9 we catch a vision of that toward which we, with God, strive:

> "They will not hurt or destroy
>   on all my holy mountain;
> for the earth will be full of the knowledge of the LORD
>   as the waters cover the sea" (11:9).

In the concluding book of the Bible the triumph of good, of God, and of God's people is celebrated. Sin and evil are no more, estrangements are healed, and the divine purpose is fulfilled:

> "See, the home of God is among mortals.
> He will dwell with them;

108

they will be his peoples,
and God himself will be with them;
he will wipe every tear from their eyes.
Death will be no more;
mourning and crying and pain will be no more,
for the first things are passed away."
    And the one who was seated on the throne said, "See I am making all things new" (Revelation 21:3-5).

A central affirmation of the Christian faith is that God has acted and continues to act throughout history to effect reconciliation and redemption. Nothing is more central to the Wesleyan tradition than this emphasis upon divine grace. Our legacy as United Methodists is the proclamation of God's grace freely available to and for all persons. In the Old Testament, God acts through the history of the chosen people—the Hebrews, the nation of Israel—to reveal the divine nature and will. The relationship between God and these people is that of covenant. A covenant is similar to a contract in that it is made between two parties and involves promises and responsibilities on both sides. Covenants to which God is a party are, of course, not between equals; they are initiated and offered by God. In Genesis 11, God enters into covenant with Abraham and with the descendants of Abraham and Sarah throughout history. God promises to be their God and claims them as God's people. Later (Genesis 17) circumcision is established as the sign of entrance into the community of the covenant people of God. Centuries later, when God delivers the Israelites from their long period of slavery in Egypt, they are guided through the desert wilderness under the leadership of Moses. At Mount Sinai (or Horeb) God communicates to them their explicit responsibilities as spelled out in the Ten Commandments and the massive legal code recorded in Exodus, Leviticus, Numbers, and Deuteronomy. This covenant at Sinai was ratified when Moses takes a basin of blood collected from sacrificial animals and throws half of it on the altar at the foot of the holy mountain and the other half upon the gathered people (Exodus 24). Throughout the Old Testament we read of Israel's commitment to live faithfully in accordance with their responsibilities as the chosen instrument through which God would bring about redemption and reconciliation. But, without exception, the Israelites are never successful in this endeavor. They fall continually and repeatedly into sin and violate their relationship with God. The cycle continues as they repent, are restored, return to sin, are punished, and repent again. Always, God's love is constant; God's faithfulness to the covenant is steadfast.

In the words of some of the prophets in the latter centuries of the Old Testament period, there is a growing realization that the people are actually incapable of keeping their side of the covenant. The sinfulness of human nature is so profound that it cannot be overcome by human intentions and efforts. Hope can rest only in the merciful action of God. In Jeremiah 31:3-33, the words of God are recorded:

> "The days are surely coming, says the LORD, when I will make a new covenant with the house of Israel and the house of Judah. . . . This is the covenant that I will make with the house of Israel after those days, says the LORD: I will put my law within them, and I will write it on their hearts; I will be their God, and they shall be my people."

This was the wonderful promise of a new act of God to make human salvation possible. The new covenant would transform the very inner being of those who would accept it and enable them to fulfill it, not by their own righteousness, but by the grace of God.

When Jesus, in the upper room with his disciples just before his arrest and crucifixion, took the cup and announced, "This cup is the new covenant in my blood," all those present recognized that what he was saying was that

110

in him the promised new covenant was becoming a reality (1 Corinthians 11:23-26). As earlier covenants had been ratified in blood, so the new covenant was sealed by the blood of the crucified Christ. (See Hebrews 8 and 9 for more on the new covenant.) The Old Testament is the story of the old covenant between God and Israel, as God attempted to reach out to all humankind with forgiveness and love. The New Testament is the story of the new covenant between God and God's people of every nation who will receive divine grace by faith. The sign of initiation into the new covenant is the sacrament of baptism. In Jesus Christ, the mediator of the new covenant, God reveals all of the divine nature and purpose that human minds can comprehend and exemplifies the highest destiny of human beings. The Christian church is the community of the new covenant—the body of Christ—charged with continuing the work of reconciling the world to God.

In Jesus Christ, God's unceasing effort to restore the goodness of the created order—begun with the Hebrews and continued by the Christian community—is brought to its climax. While we do not yet see its fullness, we know that God's victory, and ours, has been won. The image of God is restored in those who will allow themselves to be transformed. A new relationship between God and human creatures is made possible. In the Jewish Temple the focal point was the central chamber, an area that was separated from the worshipers by an ornate curtain. In this Holy of Holies, guarded by cherubim, was the ark; its top was the mercy seat. Into this chamber no one went, with the exception of the high priest who once a year took in the blood of sacrifice to atone for the sins of the people. The Holy of Holies was a place of awe, even terror, the very dwelling place of God who was remote and feared. According to Matthew 27:51, at the moment when Jesus died on the cross, "the curtain of the temple was torn in two, from top to bottom." The separation from God caused by human sin was overcome; the barrier between God and God's people was destroyed. Divine grace has made reconciliation and redemption possible.

God's Word: A Living Word

In her popular hymn "Break Thou the Bread of Life" (*The United Methodist Hymnal*, 599), Mary Lathbury says, ". . . beyond the sacred page / I seek thee, Lord; / my spirit pants for thee, / O Living Word!" These words remind us that God is not limited to pages of Scripture; God is alive and active in the world in all times and places. Our need to comprehend the way and will of God can tempt us to try to restrict God to the Bible—even to our own understanding of the Bible. This tendency to cir-cumscribe God must be resisted. As early as the third century, Tertullian is said to have chided his Christian brothers and sis-ters: "Do you think you can chase God into a book?" This is an appropriate question for us in the community of faith today. No, we cannot chase God into a book—not even into the Bible—no matter how much we might like to do so. United Methodists stand within a tradition that has always acknowledged this. We have never been a confessional church, believing that we could encapsulate truth within a creedal statement.

We cannot shrink God's revelation into a form that our finite minds can exhaust. Not only is God continuing to be active in our contemporary world, but God is also enabling us to grasp more and more of the scriptural truth that we have already received. In 1620, when the ship carrying Puritans was about to be launched, Pastor John Robinson proclaimed to his people that, "God hath more light yet to break forth from His Holy Word." In the nineteenth century, hundreds of sermons were preached from the pulpits of white churches (including many Methodist ones) justifying on specifically scriptural grounds human slavery as a fulfill-ment of the will of God. These were echoed in the twentieth century as racial segregation was justified through citation of biblical passages as the divine plan to protect the purity of the white race. In 1939, the reunion of the three largest branches of American Methodism was made possible only by the imposition of the Jim Crow system within the church with the creation of the all-black Central Jurisdiction.

A similar sorry record exists of the church's dealings with women in response to the biblical Word. In 1888, the General Conference of The Methodist Episcopal Church refused to seat Frances Willard and four other women delegates who had been elected by their annual conferences, even though the membership of the church was at that time sixty-two percent female. Full clergy rights were not extended to Methodist women until 1956, decades after secular political entities had accepted female participation. Similar examples could be multiplied endlessly. How can it possibly be claimed that we are at any point in full possession of the knowledge of God's will and purpose? How can we justify blindness to the "new light" that God has always graciously given and that we continue to receive today? We must not "seek the living among the dead," but rather strive to be receptive to the amazing grace of the Holy Spirit's continuing work, both through the unfolding of God's Word in Scripture and beyond it.

Questions for Discussion

Using Par. 63, Section 4—"Our Theological Task" in the *The Book of Discipline*, 1996, analyze the role of:
1. Scripture
2. Tradition
3. Experience
4. Reason
in our efforts as individuals and as the corporate body of the church to understand and participate in God's work in the world.

Contributors

Catherine Gunsalus González is professor of church history at Columbia Theological Seminary in Decatur, Georgia, a seminary of the Presbyterian Church (USA). She has written many Bible studies for use in churches, most recently, a commentary, *Revelation* (Louisville: Westminster/John Knox, 1997), jointly with her husband, Justo González.

Ben Witherington III is professor of New Testament interpretation at Asbury Theological Seminary in Wilmore, Kentucky. He is an elder in the Western North Carolina Annual Conference of The United Methodist Church. In 1992, he was elected a Bye Fellow of Cambridge University (Robinson College). His numerous publications include *The Jesus Quest: The Third Search for the Jew of Nazareth*, which was honored as the Biblical Studies Book of the Year by *Christianity Today* in 1995.

C. Everett Tilson is professor emeritus of Old Testament at the Methodist Theological School in Delaware, Ohio. He wrote *Segregation and the Bible*, which was lauded by an associate editor of *Ebony* magazine as "the most systematic and complete demolition . . . of segregationist arguments to appear." He has received several honors for his work for improved race relations. Since his retirement, he has coauthored seven books of litanies and other prayers for use with lectionary texts.

Gayle Carlton Felton was for years on the faculty of The Divinity School at Duke University in Durham, North Carolina, where she taught courses in Methodism and in the teaching ministry of the church. An elder in the North Carolina Annual Conference of The United Methodist Church, she is the author of two books on baptism and continues to be a leader in the church's reclaiming of the centrality of this sacrament. Presently she is a writer and consultant for worship resources with the General Board of Discipleship of The United Methodist Church in Nashville, Tennessee.

Notes

Notes to Introduction

1. *Effective Christian Education: A National Study of Protestant Congregations: A Report for The United Methodist Church* (Minneapolis: Search Institute, 1990), p. 46.

2. Ibid, p. 44.

3. For a thorough study of the 1972 and 1988 "Our Theological Task" statements and the issues involved, see Thomas A. Langford, ed., *Doctrine and Theology in The United Methodist Church*, (Nashville: Abingdon Press, 1991).

4. *The Book of Discipline of The United Methodist Church* Nashville: The United Methodist Publishing House, 1996), Par. 63.

5. *The United Methodist Hymnal* (Nashville: The United Methodist Publishing House, 1989), No. 595.

Notes to Chapter 1

1. William V. Harris, *Ancient Literacy* (Cambridge: Harvard University Press, 1989), pp. 267, 272. It was not a simple matter of class. Slaves might well be literate if they were in charge of some part of running an estate. They might also act as secretaries to their masters. Public scribes were independent, but considered low in terms of the social scale, as were shopkeepers.

2. Ibid, p. 195.

3. Justin Martyr, *First Apology*, LXVII, in *Ante-Nicene Fathers*, eds. Alexander Roberts and James Donaldson, vol. 1; (Grand Rapids: Eerdmans, 1956; reprint, no copyright given).

4. Irenaeus, *Against Heresies*, III, iv in *Ante-Nicene Fathers*, vol. 1.

5. Christopher Hibbert, *Rome: The Biography of a City* (New York: W. W. Norton, 1985), pp. 53, 74.

6. John Calvin, *The Institutes of the Christian Religion*, IV, viii.ix, trans. John Allen (Philadelphia: Westminster Press).

7. Ibid.

Notes to Chapter 2

1. I have chosen these figures because they had the most influence on American Methodism of the eighteenth and nineteenth centuries and provided the primary paradigms of how to be a student of the Bible for the early American Methodists.

2. John Wesley, "Address to the Clergy," in *The Works of John Wesley* (Grand Rapids, MI: Zondervan Publishing House, n.d.).

3. John Wesley, *Notes upon the New Testament* (New York: Lane & Scott, 1850), Preface, par. 6, p.4.

4. John Wesley, "Sermons on Several Occasions," in *Standard Sermons* (Nashville: Publishing House M.E. Church, South, n.d.), Preface, par. 5.

5. For more on Wesley's view of Scripture see my survey article "Praeparatio Evangelii: The Theological Roots of Wesley's View of Evangelism," in *Theology and Evangelism in the Wesleyan Heritage*, ed. J. C. Logan (Nashville: Abingdon Press, 1994), pp. 51–90.

6. John Wesley, *Notes*, on Colossians 3:16.

7. Ibid., Preface, par. 18.

8. Ibid., Preface.

9. L. C. Rudolph, *Francis Asbury* (Nashville: Abingdon Press, 1983), p. 141.

10. Ibid.

11. Ibid., p. 36.

12. See the letter of August 22, 1801. *The Journal and Letters of Francis Asbury: In Three Volumes*; J. Manning Potts, editor-in-chief; Elmer T. Clark, Jacob S. Payton, editors (Nashville: Abingdon Press, 1958); vol. III, p. 223. [Other references to Asbury's letters and *Journal* in this chapter are also from this source.]

13. Asbury was especially interested in the fulfillment of prophecy and so very often would study the books of Daniel and Revelation. In a *Journal* entry dated January 6-7, 1779, he spoke of having read *Prideaux's Connexcions* and "was struck with the exact fulfillment of Daniel's prophecy. 'The seventy weeks being divided into three periods,—that is, into seven, sixty-two, and one week.' " It is interesting that in most matters Asbury stayed very close to Wesley's *Notes upon the New Testament*, but unlike Wesley who had dated the end of the present kingdom of satan in 1836, Asbury pushed the date up to 1808 or 1809 (in a Letter to Thomas Douglass dated July 30, 1807). Clearly Asbury believed he was living in the shadow of the eschaton.

14. *The Journal and Letters of Francis Asbury*, vol. II, p. 270.

15. Ibid., p. 790.

16. It should be noted that the phrase "the analogy of faith" is in fact based on what is likely a frequent Protestant misreading of a key phrase from Romans 12:6, which speaks of "prophecy in proportion to [one's] faith" not "preaching according to the analogy of faith."

17. Throughout the remainder of this essay, I am quoting from Richard Watson's *Sermons and Sketches of Sermons* in two volumes pub-

lished in New York. Volume I is the 1851 edition, published by Lane & Scott; volume II, 1848, by G. Lane & C. B. Tippet. The volume and page numbers will be indicated in each case. Here it is vol. I, p. 9.

18. Ibid., p. 10.
19. Ibid., pp. 12–13.
20. Ibid., pp. 33–34.
21. Ibid., p. 165.
22. Ibid.
23. Ibid., p. 169.
24. Ibid., p. 172.
25. Ibid., vol. II, p. 194.
26. Ibid.
27. Ibid., p. 196.
28. Ibid., p. 197.
29. Notice his threefold division of Scripture into narrative, prophecy and "finally .. we have parable, allegory, and metaphor, in which we observe a peculiar display of wisdom and condescension. Illustrations are taken from natural objects, and familiar pursuits of men; and so divinely contrived, that, while the subject is illustrated by the objects to which it is compared, the objects so constantly or so frequently occurring to us may call our attention to the heavenly subject" (Ibid., p. 196).

Notes to Chapter 3

1. Gordon Kaufman, *Systematic Theology* (New York: Charles Scribner's Sons, 1968), pp. xiif.
2. Paul Minear, "The Cosmology of the Apocalypse," *Current Issues in New Testament Interpretation,* William Klassen and G. F. Snyder, eds. (New York: Harper & Bros., 1962), pp. 23–27.
3. James A. Sanders, *Torah and Canon* (Philadelphia: Fortress Press, 1972), p. 19.
4. Ibid., p. 26.
5. Ibid., p. 47.
6. Ibid., p. 52.
7. Robert Martin-Achard, *A Light to the Nations,* trans. by J. P. Smith (Edinburgh: Oliver and Boyd, 1962), p. 79.
8. *Ibid.*
9. See Wright's contribution to G. E. Wright and R. Fuller, *The Book of the Acts of God* (Garden City, NY: Doubleday and Co., Inc., 1957).
10. For a definitive presentation of the significance of this view of history for faith, see R. Bultmann, *Jesus and the Word,* tr. L. O. Smith and E. H. Lantero (New York: Charles Scribner's Sons, 1958).
11. Certainly he is not talking about David's open future, when he speaks of the Babylonian captivity as an indispensable event for understanding the whole of the Old Testament.

12. B. Davie Napier, *Song of the Vineyard* (New York: Harper & Bros., 1962), pp. 3–9.

13. H. P. Rickman, *Meaning in History* (London: George Allen & Unwin Ltd., 1961), p. 60, asserts of Dilthey.

14. Gregory Dix, *Jew and Greek* (Philadelphia: Dacre Press, 1953), p. 79.

15. Nels Ferré, *The Universal Word* (Philadelphia: The Westminster Press, 1969).

16. Karl Rahner, "Theology and Anthropology," *The Word in History*, T. P. Burke, ed., (New York: Sheed and Ward, Inc., 1966), p. 21.

Notes to Chapter 4

1. Archibald A. Hodge and Benjamin B. Warfield, "Inspiration," *Presbyterian Review*, II (1881), p. 238.

2. J. Philip Wogaman, *Circuit Rider*, April 1994, pp. 4-5.

3. Ibid.

4. Leander E. Keck, ed., *The New Interpreter's Bible*, vol. 1 (Nashville: Abingdon Press, 1994), p. 150. Massey's article is followed by ones from writers representing African American, Asian American, Hispanic American, Native American, and women's perspectives. This volume also includes other articles that are very helpful in our task of scriptural interpretation.

Printed in the United States
18785LVS00001B/217-381